BATTLEFIELDS
IN MINIATURE

Battlefields In Miniature

Making Realistic and Effective Terrain for Wargames

Paul Davies

Pen & Sword
MILITARY

First published in Great Britain in 2015 by
Pen & Sword Military
an imprint of
Pen & Sword Books Ltd
47 Church Street
Barnsley
South Yorkshire
S70 2AS

ISBN 978 1 78159 274 8

Typeset in Ehrhardt by
Mac Style Ltd, Bridlington, East Yorkshire
Printed and bound in India by Replika Press Pvt. Ltd.

Pen & Sword Books Ltd incorporates the imprints of Pen & Sword
Archaeology, Atlas, Aviation, Battleground, Discovery, Family History,
History, Maritime, Military, Naval, Politics, Railways, Select, Transport,
True Crime, and Fiction, Frontline Books, Leo Cooper, Praetorian Press,
Seaforth Publishing and Wharncliffe.

For a complete list of Pen & Sword titles please contact
PEN & SWORD BOOKS LIMITED
47 Church Street, Barnsley, South Yorkshire, S70 2AS, England
E-mail: enquiries@pen-and-sword.co.uk
Website: www.pen-and-sword.co.uk

CONTENTS

ABOUT THE AUTHOR

Paul Davies has been a wargamer – or as his long-suffering wife prefers to say, has been 'messing around with toy soldiers and all that malarkey' – for more years than he cares to admit or chooses to remember. Suffice to say that when Airfix released their Guards colour party plastic figures, he was at the front of the queue outside his local toyshop. The wargaming possibilities of this set were somewhat limited, and suitable plastic opponents non-existent, but as soon as the British infantry combat group were released, followed by German infantry, he never looked back; he still harbours an affection for soft plastic even though that view seems to be tantamount to heresy in some quarters.

Allegedly, the hobby has kept him relatively sane, and he has been a regular contributor to *Wargames Illustrated* since 2006, and in 2008 wrote the first of a regular series of 'How to…' articles aimed at showing wargamers of different skill levels how to construct their own buildings and terrain features. In addition to his magazine work, he also undertakes private commissions for individual wargamers and clubs, winning numerous awards, including in 2008 the Best Terrain award at Salute for his 1/300th scale interpretation of the Battle of the Alma!

Paul lives with his wife and son in Minehead in Somerset where he continues to wargame at his local club, design and construct buildings and terrain, write magazine articles and reviews, and no doubt, if asked, further books.

Introduction

E ver since 2008, when I wrote my first 'How to...' article for *Wargames Illustrated*, I've often been asked if I would ever write a book about making wargame terrain and scenery. To be honest, I'd thought about it, but the time just hadn't been right. However now, thanks to Pen & Sword, I've finally got my act together and written this book to help you to make your own terrain and scenery, from simple to more complex projects which broadly span historical periods and geographical locations, as well as being suitable for fantasy and sci-fi gaming.

Before going any further I should clarify some of the terminology used:

- Terrain is the 'ground' onto which I place scenery. Depending on the way in which you decide to create your terrain it may also include natural or man-made features like rivers and roads.
- Scenery comprises of whatever I place onto the terrain; rivers, hills, trees etc., and man-made objects such as roads, fences, walls, bridges and of course buildings.

I've occasionally been asked, 'Why bother with terrain and scenery anyway?' My answer is to adapt Frederick the Great's observation that artillery lends dignity to what might otherwise be a vulgar brawl, by suggesting that terrain and scenery lend interest to what might otherwise be just a boring table, with the caveat that although realistic terrain undoubtedly enhances the wargame experience, it's not essential for an enjoyable game.

As a keen wargamer who moved into the hobby from modelmaking, aesthetics are very important to me, and I do prefer fighting battles on well-prepared terrain, with well-painted miniatures. Like railway modellers who every so often get down to track level to view their creation, it is not unknown for me to, part way through a game, take a look at the battle from 'ground level' to view the action. And when taking photographs at wargame shows for *Wargames Illustrated* I always try to do so (Figures 1–2).

I always prefer to see wargame figures set into the terrain rather than on it, and another good example of this approach is the 15mm *Wagram* game presented by Gary Williams and Martin Stanbridge of the Loughton Strike Force (Figure 3).

INTRODUCTION

Figure 3:
Wagram in 15mm.
*(Gary Williams and
Martin Stanbridge)*

When considering whether or not to make your own scenery, there are a number of considerations to take into account, not least financial and time constraints. Whether you buy or make your terrain and scenery there is always a cost involved, and it would be misleading of me to claim that making your own terrain will always save you money. Sometimes it will, sometimes it won't, but what it will always do is give you the opportunity to create your own unique wargaming experience by giving you total creative control. With practice and experience, you will be able to make exactly what you need and not be restricted by what is available commercially. Having said that, there is a tremendous range of terrain and buildings available across the scales, much of it is reasonably priced so long as you don't want too much of it, and you can always adapt it to make it more individual to you (Figure 4).

Time too can sometimes be an issue. Creating your own collection of terrain and scenery won't happen overnight, and you should never rush terrain and scenery making: that's when things go horribly wrong as I know to my cost from working on modelmaking commissions with unrealistically short deadlines. Admittedly sometimes you can have a happy accident and discover a new technique; I've had a few of those which I'll mention later but generally, rushing and trusting to luck shouldn't be seen as an acceptable modelmaking technique!

Figure 4:
This building has been adapted from two 4Ground originals by Mark Densham to create a unique model.

Figure 5:
Prussian *Dystopian Wars* sea and air forces head off to battle on a photographic background cloth.

INTRODUCTION

Returning to the aesthetics of terrain, although I enjoy playing on well presented and visually pleasing terrain, or amongst authentic looking buildings, these shouldn't be considered as a guarantee of a good game. I have experienced many highly enjoyable games using minimal terrain (Figure 5).

For me, an enjoyable game needs several elements: good company, a challenging scenario, sensible rules, well-painted models and the right terrain. And a few decent dice rolls once in a while would come in handy too!

This book will help you to create the terrain and scenery that will realistically meet your needs, but these practical projects are just a starting point, and whether you simply follow them, or are inspired to create your own, I hope that this book will increase your enjoyment of what is for me a really great hobby, whether you refight battles from history or from the worlds of fantasy or science fiction.

A peaceful medieval scene. (*Minehead Wargames Club*)

Welcome to the Workshop

1

For anyone thinking about making their own terrain and scenery for the first time, this chapter provides an overview of the basic tools you need to get started, as well as a few specialist tools to make your modelmaking life easier (although they're not essential). As a general rule, always buy the best tools you can afford.

If you are already a keen modelmaker, your first impulse will probably be to skip over this chapter, but I'd urge you to stick with it, because I mention some very useful tools and materials that you might not have seen before.

But before reading any further, let's run through the mandatory health and safety warnings:

- Sharp things can cut you.
- Hot things can burn you.
- Anything that gives off a vapour may make you ill, nauseous or worse.
- Wear a facemask when using fine materials such as static grass.
- Whenever possible, use aerosol paints outside … but check which way the wind is blowing first! And as an aside, be aware that aerosol paints don't produce good results when used in low temperatures.
- Finally, always read and follow manufacturers' instructions.

Even if you are an experienced and careful modelmaker, accidents can and do happen. I managed to sever an artery in my leg with a 10A scalpel blade! I won't bore you with the details, other than to recommend that you keep a first aid box close to your workbench, or at least know where the plasters are kept. Admittedly plasters didn't prove effective when fighting an arterial bleed: I had to wrap my leg tightly with a tea towel and then drive 10 miles to the nearest hospital, but on the positive side I managed to convince the nurse to let me have the suturing tweezers used to sew me up. Would you believe these precision instruments were being thrown away after a single use? And as well as doing a good job stitching me back together, they are perfect for rigging model sailing ships (Figure 6).

Throughout this book I've used metric measurements wherever possible to keep things simple and streamlined; if you wish to measure in feet and inches, the following approximate conversions will come in handy:

- 2.5cm = 1 inch
- 30cm = 12 inches

Figure 6:
Adding rigging to a
Sails of Glory HMS
Defence.

Figure 6:
Adding rigging to a *Sails of Glory* HMS *Defence.*

Your Main Armoury

The tools suggested in this section are useful, but you don't need to buy them all at once; you'll probably already have quite a few useful tools, such as scissors or tweezers etc. And as you make more terrain and scenery your collection of tools and equipment will grow.

To make it as easy as possible to look at the tools you might need, I've grouped them according to their primary function.

MEASURING AND MARKING OUT

Steel rules are essential both for measuring and as a cutting guide. It's useful to have both 15cm and 30cm rulers. The 15cm rule comes in very useful when working in a confined space or cutting out small components.

Probably the most useful metal ruler I have found is the Maun Safety Ruler (Figure 7). The unique shallow 'M' cross section helps protect your valuable digits from being accidently sliced and joining the scrap pile.

When making buildings you'll invariably need to create accurate right angles for which I use a basic engineers' square. For more options, a combination square allows you to create precise 45° angles.

Figure 7:
The Maun Safety
Ruler.

CUTTING

One of the most commonly used (and sharpest) cutting tools is the scalpel blade. I use Swann Morton surgical blades because they have a wide range of blade shapes, although over time I seem to have standardised on their 10A blade. Swann Morton also produces compatible blade handles. Obviously there are other scalpel blade and handle manufacturers, but always buy your blades and handles from the same manufacturer, and never buy handles that have a round cross section (Figure 8), because if your work surface isn't perfectly flat they can roll – usually towards you – and drop off the surface and probably into your foot!

Depending upon the blade handle design, fitting and removing the blade can be tricky. My method is to hold the blade in a pair of pliers and carefully slide it into position (Figure 9); removal is the reverse procedure. Whichever method you use, be careful. There's a very good reason why they're called surgical blades: they are very, very sharp!

Another cutting option is the single sided razor blade, which I use mainly for cutting stripwood or matchsticks. There are also various types of craft knives, from the heavy duty Stanley knife to snap-off blade knives. I tend to use the latter with the blade fully extended when cutting through high density foam … it causes less problems at home than using our best carving knife!

3

Figure 8:
The right and wrong design of scalpel blade handles.

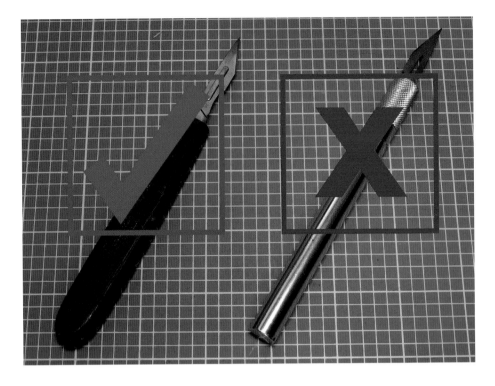

Figure 9:
The safe way to fit a scalpel blade.

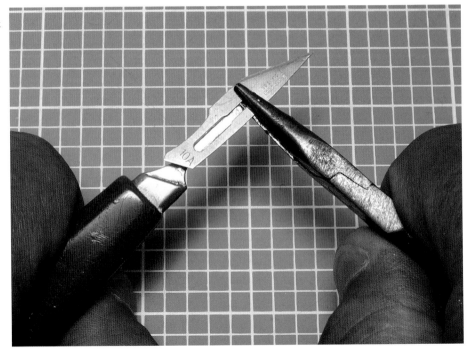

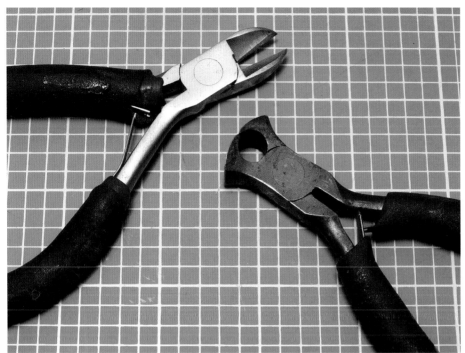

Whichever type of knife you use, to ensure the cleanest cut and protect your work surface, you'll need a self-healing cutting mat.

I also use various types of cutters (Figure 10) to remove components from their plastic sprue prior to cleaning up the components with a fine file or an emery stick. And if you anticipate building palisades, log cabins or similar structures for which you'll be using barbeque skewers or bamboo, you'll need a pair of garden secateurs; my secateurs had extensive use when I created a palisade and buildings for an Arthurian demonstration game (Figure 11).

Another unusual but very useful cutting tool is a circle cutter. Mine is made by Ohnar and has given long service; the only downside is that it can be difficult to obtain the blades, so whichever brand of circle cutter you choose, make sure you buy plenty of spare blades. As well as cutting accurate circles, I also use it to mark out roads. Simply extend the circle cutter to the appropriate width and then carefully trace out the shape of road. The blade and the needle will leave two feint parallel lines that are good enough to provide a cutting guide.

When making terrain, you'll almost certainly be working with high density foam which is sold in many different forms and under various trade names including Styrofoam®, Polyfoam®, Craftfoam® and Reticel®. It's available in different sheet sizes, thicknesses and densities; generally the densest is

Figure 11:
Age of Arthur
demonstration
game.
(*The Crawley
Wargames Club*)

best, but it's also the most expensive. In my experience, it's a good idea to adapt the size of your intended terrain panels to match available sheet sizes because it can be difficult to cut the material accurately yourself. However for cutting or shaping pieces for specific terrain features like hills or cliffs, a useful tool is a compass saw (which is basically a hacksaw blade in a handle).

For the sake of household harmony, remember that cutting high density foam makes a mess that some vacuum cleaners stubbornly refuse to suck up. You should also wear a facemask when cutting this material because you really don't want to inhale the dust (and the same applies when cutting mdf).

Remaining with the subject of high density foam, one of the most useful tools I've ever bought is the Peter Child Artist's Pyrography machine. This is basically a mains transformer that controls the heat passing through a thin piece of wire shaped to create a nib-like tool for engraving into a suitable surface or bent to create cutting profiles. You can see the tool in use later in the book in the *Wings of Glory* project in Chapter Six. This tool is easily the most expensive that I have bought, but it still works perfectly after more than 15 years, proving that if you buy the best you get your monies worth.

DRILLING

A mains-powered modelmaking drill can be useful, and good ones are produced by Dremel® and Minicraft®. Whichever brand you purchase, make sure that it has a slow speed setting for precise work. Another useful tool for drilling is a hand-operated pin vice. They're cheap and easily controllable. As well as general modelmaking, I also use mine for drilling out the hands of figures to replace lances or pikes.

FILING

You'll need a selection of fine needle files for finishing off surfaces. To remove the waste material that can clog up the file you'll also need a brass suede brush: buy brass because it's a soft metal and is less likely to damage the file.

GRIPPING

Inevitably you'll have assemblies that need to be held tightly in position whilst glue is setting. You don't need anything sophisticated and I've collected a random mix of pegs, bulldog clips, cheap clamps and elastic bands that work just fine.

Occasionally when making buildings, and certainly when painting miniatures, you get those moments when you wish you had another hand or two. Fortunately, help is available in the form of the aptly named Helping Hands tool consisting of a beam with a crocodile clip clamp at each end, securely supported on a heavyweight base (Figure 12). Some versions include an integral magnifying glass.

Although I use mine in modelmaking, I find it particularly useful when painting figures. My rationale is simple: if the hand holding the paintbrush is shaking and the hand holding the figure or base is also shaking then you're making your life twice as difficult as you need to.

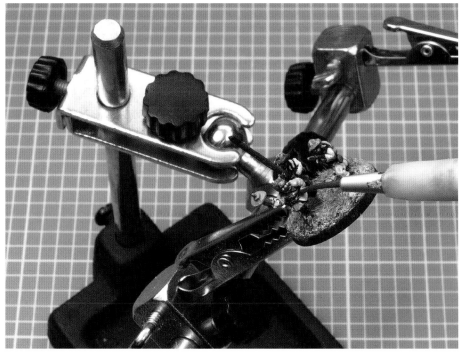

Figure 12:
You never know when an extra pair of hands will be useful!

Additional Tools

HOT MELT GLUE GUN

For those times when conventional glues just don't seem to work, hot wax will often do the job but you'll need a suitable glue gun. Remember that hot wax is … hot, so take care.

LEGO® BRICKS

Not strictly tools, but I have used them for many years as an aid to creating right angles for buildings. Mine cost me next to nothing.

STATIC GRASS APPLICATOR

I use static grass in terrain and scenery making, and also on the bases of my figures and movement trays (Figure 13). It can be applied in several ways, primarily depending on the area that needs to be covered. For small areas I use a simple (and cheap) puffer bottle. You simply apply PVA glue in the appropriate areas, shake the puffer to create some static charge and then puff the grass onto the glue.

When grassing figure bases, it can help to make the grass stand up if you invert the base and lightly tap the underside. I've also heard of modelmakers who hold the base close to a CRT TV; the static electricity from the screen attracts the static grass fibres pulling them upright and away from the base.

Figure 13:
Static grass applied to bases.

8

Figure 14:
A grassy bank created using the pinch and glue technique.

Another technique that works reasonably well is to apply PVA glue and then pinch up a clump of static grass and push it into the PVA (Figure 14). The pinching tends to squeeze the fibres upright. Once the glue has dried thoroughly, turn the base upside down and tap the base so that any static grass that hasn't been glued can be collected up and used later. When using this technique, keep your fingers moist otherwise the static grass will stick to your fingers instead of the base. I used this technique for the ramparts of the hill fort project in Chapter Seventeen.

For covering larger areas of terrain I use a tool much favoured by the railway modelling fraternity: an electro-static applicator such as The Flockit produced by Green Scene, which although relatively expensive at around £75, has a lifetime no-quibble guarantee and it works extremely well. Simply fill the container with static grass and then apply PVA glue to the area to be covered. Next clip one end of the earth wire to the glued area. Turn it on and shake the device over the glued area and the static grass will stand proud.

CREATING YOUR OWN TUFTS

There are several companies selling ready-made tufts but if you have your own electro-static grass machine, you can make your own (Figure 15). You can choose from different colours and lengths of fibre to create exactly the tufts you need. I must be honest, mine are not as neat as those you can buy,

but it doesn't really matter. I just squirt several blobs of PVA onto a piece of clear acetate, spread it around a bit using a cocktail stick, and then use my electro-static grass machine as previously described. Leave it overnight, and then turn the acetate upside down and give it a gentle tap to dislodge the static grass that hasn't been glued.

I bring into service all sorts of scrap acetate from packaging to the clear lids used on yoghurt cartons. Remember, the first rule of terrain and scenery making: throw nothing away!

Before leaving the subject of static grass I recommend that when you are using it, you wear a mask of some sort, because the fibres are extremely fine and light, and tend to float around in the air and be easily inhaled (which can cause an allergic reaction).

AIRBRUSH

This is one of those pieces of equipment that you never feel you need until you get one, and then you can't believe how you managed to get along without it. Why bother with an airbrush when there are so many different colours available in aerosol spray cans? A fair question, and for me, there are many reasons:

- Spray cans are expensive, and if you use them a lot an airbrush will save you money in the long run (even allowing for the initial cost of the airbrush and a small compressor).

- An airbrush is much easier to control than an aerosol can.
- Aerosol spray cans can only spray at a set width, so if you're spraying a small area you waste a lot of paint in overspray; a good quality airbrush can spray a line as narrow as 0.16mm, so there's minimal overspray and wastage.
- Sometimes aerosol sprays attack foam, which can be a serious problem if you use foam in the construction of your terrain or buildings; I've never had that problem when using an airbrush.
- An airbrush is far more environmentally friendly and safer than spray cans because it uses compressed air as a propellant rather than flammable gaseous propellants.
- Although there are a lot of different coloured aerosol sprays available, with an airbrush there is no limit to the colour choices available to you.

In short an airbrush saves me money and increases the instances when I can benefit from using a spray.

There are a lot of decisions to be made when selecting the airbrush that is right for your particular needs. I would recommend studying the websites of companies such as Badger, Iwata, Paasche and Aztek for the most up-to-date information. As a starting point, always look for a modellers' airbrush, not one aimed at artists or illustrators because they are designed to use very thin paints and inks that won't be any use for modelling applications.

For me, the most important decision was whether to buy a single action or a dual action airbrush. A single action airbrush means that you adjust the width of the spray using one control and then spray using the trigger. A dual action airbrush has a trigger that allows you to simultaneously spray and, by sliding it forward or back, vary the thickness of the spray. In the end, I chose a single action Badger 200NH model because I couldn't envisage any situations in which I would need to vary the thickness of my sprayed line during the spraying process … and a single action model was cheaper than a dual action model. This particular airbrush has an adjustable spray from 0.16mm to 50mm, which is more than adequate for my terrain and scenery making needs as well as being suitable for spraying my figures too.

Although this section is about the merits of using an airbrush over aerosol cans, I feel that I should share an additional problem I've encountered when using spray cans, and that is the difference between primer spray and colour spray. The purpose of a primer is to create a surface onto which the topcoat can adhere. To achieve this, the primer dries with a slightly roughened surface to which the top coat can better grip. All very sensible but if, for example, you decide to use a grey primer as the coat for say, a small scale naval vessel, you will have a problem because of the primer's rough finish (Figure 16). Sadly the result was a ruined model, and at £10 that was no joke, so learn from my mistake.

Figure 16: Why
you shouldn't use
primer as a colour.

Figure 16: Why you shouldn't use primer as a colour.

OPTIVISOR

For detail work I find that a magnifying glass is too awkward. Instead I bought an Optivisor several years ago. The unit fits around your head and has a choice of lenses that slot inside the visor, each with different degrees of magnification. There is also a version with an integral light, but in my experience it's better to have the light source separate because it allows more flexibility when you position it.

Materials

It's impossible to list every material that you may find yourself using in the course of your terrain and scenery making, but each project in this book includes a list of the materials needed, and the following selection highlights the materials I use most often in my terrain building.

HIGH DENSITY FOAM

This is the generic term for extruded polystyrene (XPS), which is marketed under a variety of trade names such as Polyfoam®, Recticel®, Styrofoam® and Craftfoam®. It is not the same as the expanded polystyrene that is used in packaging. The latter can be used for creating small hills so long as they're coated with PVA glue to toughen up the surface, but even so, I would recommend that you steer clear of expanded polystyrene because it is too fragile for the regular handling associated with wargaming use.

One cautionary note regarding Polyfoam and Recticel: these materials are generally sold in sizes to fit between roof joists, namely about 120cm x 50cm x 6cm. Most wargaming terrain tile systems are based on multiples of 60cm square tiles or 120cm x 60cm, which means that the tiles can be rotated through 360° to create different configurations. If you use materials that are either not square or with the length not exactly double the width, you will find that they are not as versatile as other high density foam materials. I use various brands of high density foam for my terrain, such as those named above, but for simplicity I will just describe them as 'high density foam'.

My first stop for sourcing this material is from a builders' merchant, where you can check the material before buying. Having said that, if you discover a particular online supplier who has the right product at the right price, then use them. For example, I now buy virtually all my high density foam from Panel Systems who manufacture the materials to different sizes and density, and although I have to buy relatively large quantities, it works out cheaper per individual sheet than buying from model shops. Generally the denser the material the stronger it is, but also the more expensive; always try to buy the best materials you can afford when building terrain because you want it to give many years' service.

As well as being available in thick blocks, which are ideal for terrain, you can also buy thinner sheets around 0.3cm or 0.5cm thick that can be useful when constructing buildings and other man-made structures. You can lightly engrave stonework or brick courses into the surface of the high density foam using an old ballpoint pen (Figure 17).

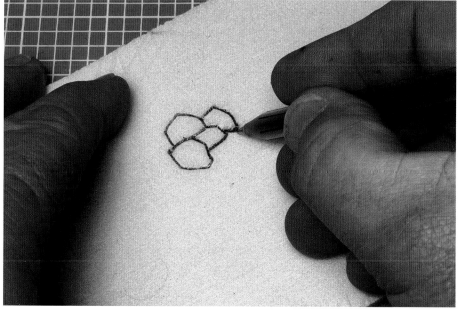

Figure 17:
Engraving
stonework into
high density foam.

FOAMBOARD OR FOAMCORE

This material was originally used for mounting photographs or prints, but its lightness, strength and dimensional stability soon brought it to the attention of modelmakers. It comprises a thin layer of foam, usually 0.3cm or 0.5cm, sandwiched between white or black paper. The surface of this material is very smooth so any texture required will have to be created. Such texture is usually added either by applying a coating of PVA and fine sand, or by adding a thin coating of filler. Another popular technique is to spread a thin layer of air-drying clay onto the surface and then engraving stone or brickwork (Figure 18).

Figure 18:
Stonework engraved into a layer of air-drying clay on a foamboard wall.

CORK TILES

Cork tiles are often used as an alternative to high density foamboard when making buildings, because cork has an interesting surface texture which can make areas of otherwise blank wall look more interesting without needing to apply a texture coating.

WOOD

I believe that if you want to represent wood in modelmaking, you should use wood. So I always have stocks of different thickness balsa sheet and stripwood, as well as veneer, barbeque skewers, broken bamboo roller blinds, cocktail sticks and toothpicks. I use both cocktail sticks and toothpicks because I find that the latter are less regular and rougher looking than cocktail sticks, making them more suitable for rustic fencing.

FAKE FUR

This is probably the most frequently used material for representing thatch. The thatch creating technique is relatively messy, as projects featured later in this book will show, but I think it's worth the effort (Figure 19).

Figure 19:
A fake fur thatched roof.

OTHER MATERIALS

There are many more materials that I use, and which you'll discover for yourself as you make more models. You'll also develop an eye for spotting the modelmaking possibilities in totally unconnected products. For example, whilst scouting around a local hardware store, I spotted a couple of sink drainers. Now everyone else just saw sink drainers, but I saw the outlets for a rocket engine! What makes this worse is that I seriously doubt whether I'll ever need to build a rocket engine or anything vaguely similar, but if I do...

As a cautionary note, as you start to accumulate all manner of bits and pieces for future use, try to store them somewhere that they can be found at a later date.

The following table sums up the materials I use most frequently, as well as some others that I've found useful. This list really is just the start, and you will probably discover other or alternative materials; if you do, remember to share your finds and ideas with other wargamers, and hopefully they will do the same.

Material	Uses
Aluminium mesh	The diamond shaped mesh is good for creating leaded windows.
Balsa	The best way to represent wood. Available in sheets or strips.
Barbeque skewers	Useful for palisades or log building. Usually easier to cut than bamboo and garden canes.
Broom heads	The bristles make good reeds.
Cocktail sticks and toothpicks	Ideal as the basis for different types of fences, also for holding high density foam assemblies. Toothpicks have a rougher, more natural look.
Coconut fibre doormat	Used to represent fields with growing crops. Sometimes it's cut into pieces the same width as figure bases so that sections can be removed as the troops make their way through the field, which looks much better than figures standing on top of the crops.
Coir basket liner	Thin sheets of coconut fibre that can be used to simulate thatch.
Cork bark	A good way to represent rugged cliff faces. Quite difficult to obtain: try florists or pet shops.
Cork tiles	An alternative to using foam for walls and has an interesting texture.
Corrugated card	Good for simulating pantile roofs. I use cat food cartons and strip away the outer surface by lightly soaking it with water and leaving the card to dry.
Dried herbs	Good for ground cover.
Fake fur	The best material for creating thatch. Larger pieces can make excellent terrain cloths.
High density foam	Sold under various brand names, probably the most widely used material for terrain building.
Foamboard/foamcore	Used for building construction. Be careful if using it for small scale buildings as the exposed width of the material around windows and doors may look over-scale.
Green pan scourers	Can be used to make small scale hedges, or natural roofs for small buildings.
Rubberised horsehair	Originally intended for stuffing upholstery, this material is commonly used as the basis for the foliage of deciduous trees and large hedges.
Textured and blown wallpaper	Can be used to represent random stonework or cobbled streets depending on the pattern.
Wet-and-dry paper	When glued to a rigid base, wet-and-dry makes a passable tarmac road. Don't be tempted to use ordinary sand or glasspaper. When they get wet the gritty surface disintegrates. Wet-and-dry is formulated to withstand a certain amount of water (or paint).

Adhesives

Unsurprisingly, the more materials you use, the more types of adhesive you'll need to be familiar with. My general rule is to ask advice, whether from where you obtain your materials or from other wargamers. Always read the manufacturers' instructions, but if in any doubt, test every material and adhesive combination before working on the actual project. A bit of caution at this stage will save a lot of heartache later.

The following table provides a guide to the most commonly used materials and adhesives that I have used successfully.

Material	Adhesive	Comments
Balsa wood	Balsa cement. You can also use superglue if you're in a hurry	There is a temptation when using wood, to use stains and varnishes. If you do, be sparing in how you apply glue because it can leave a skin over the wood that will affect the coverage of any stain.
Card and paper	PVA (white glue)	Always buy undiluted PVA, and dilute it as required. Allow plenty of drying time.
Expanded polystyrene packaging	Tile adhesive or instant grab adhesive such as No More Nails®	I've specified 'packaging' because this type of expanded polystyrene is manufactured to different standards and qualities. Whichever glue you use, run a test first.
Plasticard	Slater's Mekpak®	I had many some frustrating experiences making Plasticard models until I used Mekpak.
Plastic kits	Polystyrene cement	Buy the ones with a fine needle nozzle for maximum control.
Polyfoam, Reticel or Styrofoam	PVA (white glue) or instant grab adhesive	Styrofoam or high density foam is the material most often used for making terrain. I have had good results with both glue options, but, just to be sure, I always pin pieces together using cocktail sticks for extra strength.
Resin	Superglue	I use the gel version because it has some gap filling properties that can be useful.
Stones	Superglue or hot melt glue	For small stones such as those that you might use to aid detail to a base, I use superglue but for larger areas I use hot melt glue.
Wood	PVA (white) glue	Always allow plenty of drying time when using PVA glue and if possible, clamp components together for the entire drying time.

I couldn't end this basic list of adhesives without mentioning Milliput®. Originally formulated for DIY and plumbing repairs, this epoxy putty was eagerly grasped by the modelmaking community. It can be used for modelling and sculpting and also adheres to almost any surface making it a combination of modelling clay and glue. Once dry it can be cut, sanded, shaped and painted, and it's available in several different grades. It takes a bit of practice to use, but once you are familiar with it, this is probably one of the most versatile modelling materials you will find.

Do remember that when using adhesives, many of them give off unpleasant vapours, so always work in well ventilated areas and ideally wear a mask.

2

WHAT'S EVERYONE ELSE DOING?

Before making a start on building your own terrain, it's a good idea to take a look at what other wargamers are doing, because this can save you both time and money. Ideally, visit as many wargame shows as you can and talk to other wargamers, who in my experience are always happy to share their terrain making experiences, both good and bad. Always learn from your mistakes and from those of others. After all, there are an infinite number of new mistakes to make, so why repeat old ones?

Ultimately all terrain making involves a compromise between aesthetic appearance, playability, storage and cost, and it's up to each wargamer to decide on his or her priorities. This chapter presents a brief overview of just some of the examples of different types of terrain you'll see around the show circuit. In the following chapters I'll look in more detail at how you can make your own.

Cloth on the Table

For most wargamers of a certain age, their introduction to the hobby started with a green cloth laid over some books to create contours, some trees made from bits of sponge on a stick, a few buildings and a couple of armies. The material choices for terrain cloths has increased in the past five or so years, and for me this remains the most flexible and generally cost-effective terrain system.

Richard Gillingham is a keen and successful user of the terrain cloth, and capitalises on its lightness and ease of transportation. He took his game *Okeechobee* to Salute, one of the UK's premier wargame shows, making a round trip of more than 400 miles via rail and underground, with everything packed into a single rucksack! Mind you, it was clearly worth the effort because *Okeechobee* won the well-deserved prize for The Most Completely Realised Game of the show (Figure 20).

When choosing the material to use for your terrain cloth, even if you're going to cover most of it with scatter material such as lichen and sponge, it's a good idea to pick a material that doesn't crease. There's nothing better guaranteed to spoil the look of a game, than a terrain cloth with unmistakeable creases all over it. For example, felt will crease but fleece (which looks similar), doesn't. Fleece is therefore my first choice for a naval terrain cloth, particularly if you don't want to spend much money on terrain because you're just dipping your toe in the water of naval wargaming (Figure 21). Sorry about the pun: I just couldn't help myself.

Figure 20:
Okeechobee.
(Richard Gillingham)

Figure 21: *Sails of Glory* Napoleonic ships battle it out on a sea of blue-grey fleece.

And there is a case to suggest that if you put enough ground cover, figures, roads, buildings and trees on your terrain cloth, you won't actually see much of it anyway (Figure 22), as was the case with the highly detailed game *Winter of Discontent* by the Very British Civil War Forum and the Exmouth Imperials.

One of the most popular materials for terrain cloths is fake fur, which was used to very good effect by the South East Essex Military Society (SEEMS), whose *War of the Spanish Succession* game won the trophy for best game at Battlegroup South, Bovington (Figure 23). The fake fur was dyed to vary the colour and roads were created by cutting away the fur, coating with flexible bathroom sealant and painting. To save time you can buy flexible sealant that is brown and so cut out the painting step. The hills were made by placing suitably shaped high density foam hills underneath the terrain cloth.

Fake fur isn't only used to create a complete terrain cloth. The Loughton Strike Force used a small section of it, to represent a lush cornfield in their *Waterloo* game (Figure 24). Another way of using fake fur is to cut it into squares or rectangles and dye or paint it different colours to represent different crops as was done by the Skirmish Wargamers, with their *Barkesdale's Charge: Gettysburg* (Figure 25). A similar material to fake fur is the throw, which usually has a different length of fur on each side to offer more variety and choice.

Figure 23:
War of the Spanish Succession game.
(*The South East Essex Military Society*)

Figure 24:
A British square awaits the French cavalry at *Waterloo*.
(*The Loughton Strike Force*)

Figure 25:
*Barkesdale's
Charge: Gettysburg.
(The Skirmish
Wargamers)*

Figure 26:
Electric hair
clippers at work.

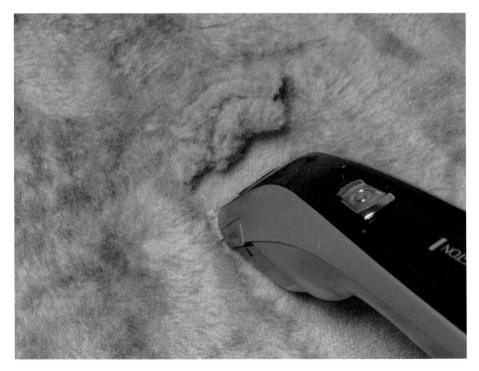

Figure 27:
Franco-Prussian War.
(Nik Harwood)

You can use shorter length fur when using small scale figures, and longer lengths for larger figures; an integral road network may be created by using a pair of electric hair clippers to cut away the fur (Figure 26). Once the fur is completely cut back, the road can be painted, the cloth spread out on a table and let battle commence, as The Minehead Wargames Club did with their *Franco-Prussian War* game using 10mm Pendraken figures (Figure 27).

Whatever base material you use for your terrain cloth, it's unlikely that you'll want to use the cloth as purchased. You can randomly dye your cloth, or you can spray it using different coloured matt aerosol sprays. The playing surface can be further enhanced by adding clumps of lichen or coloured sponge – even small pebbles or shingle – depending on the geography depicted. I've concentrated on grassy, temperate terrain primarily because it offers the widest gaming potential, but the same principles apply to other types of terrain, whether arid desert, snow or even sea: you start with a suitably coloured material onto which is added various details.

You can also adapt other materials to create interesting gaming mats. For example Ian Wood used a large sheet of leathercloth to represent the urban terrain in his *Infinity* game (Figure 28).

Often a combination of terrain systems can be used advantageously such as with *Up the Nile Without a Paddle* presented by the Southend Wargames Club, where sculpted terrain panels were laid over a cloth to create the Nile (Figure 29). One advantage of this approach is that it's easy to reduce or increase the width of your river, without having to buy or make additional terrain panels.

Figure 28:
An interesting way
to solve a parking
problem in *Infinity*.
(*Ian Wood*)

Figure 29:
*Up the Nile Without
a Paddle*.
(*The Southend
Wargames Club*)

Gaming Mats

As a development of the terrain cloth, you can also buy specifically produced gaming mats or cloths, but you need to be cautious because some of them crease easily (which is the last thing you want). The most important property of a gaming mat is that it doesn't crease when it is put away after a game. Be wary of buying grass mats; these are mainly produced for railway modellers and are intended to be glued permanently onto terrain or over hills, and are definitely not designed to be repeatedly rolled or folded.

The *American War of Independence* battle by the Wessex Wyverns used a gaming mat as the basis for the terrain (Figure 30). Green felt pieces were used to show the edges of the woodland areas. Defining the edges of woodland, particularly woodland that restricts movement or visibility, is important and can be a problem when using individually based trees. A piece of green felt solves the problem, and it can always be made less obvious by sprinkling it with pieces of lichen, and small pebbles may be used to define any passable routes through the trees.

There are several specialist manufacturers producing gaming mats to suit almost any wargaming location or scenario. For example, Hotz Artworks in the USA produce the Hotz Mat in a variety of finishes including fields, First World War trenches, a Wild West town, even a water-filled gladiatorial arena! The Air Combat Group used a partially repainted Hotz hex mat for their Vietnam Air War game, *Feet Wet, Feet Dry* (Figure 31).

Figure 30:
American War of Independence battle on a gaming mat.
(*The Wessex Wyverns*)

Figure 31:
Feet Wet, Feet Dry,
a Vietnam airwar
game.
*(The Air Combat
Group)*

Terrain Mat

A variation on the terrain cloth and gaming mat is the commercially produced terrain mat. These occupy a particular niche in wargame terrain as they fall somewhere between a gaming mat and sculpted terrain. One of the best manufacturers of terrain mats is named Terrain Mat, who produce an extensive range of textures. Apart from the usual temperate and arid terrain needs, they also produce terrain mats for specific campaigns such as the First World War Western Front, the Battle of Britain, the D-Day landings and even galactic space. My particular favourite is their sea mat to which has been added a clear but non-intrusive hex grid (Figure 32).

TERRAIN TILES

I think almost every wargamer either has, or has played on, terrain tiles. Usually 60cm square, about 5cm deep and coated with static grass or flock, they come in a variety of configurations with integrated roads, water features and much more.

The *English Civil War* by Phil and Steve Deeprose used terrain tiles and hills, with some pieces of doormat to represent cornfields, to create a fast moving game (Figure 33).

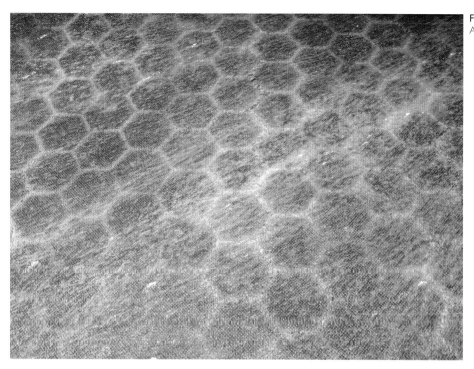

Figure 32:
A sea terrain mat.

Figure 33:
English Civil War at
Battlegroup South,
Bovington Tank
Museum.
(*Phil and Steve
Deeprose*)

Figure 34:
TSS terrain tile
cross section.

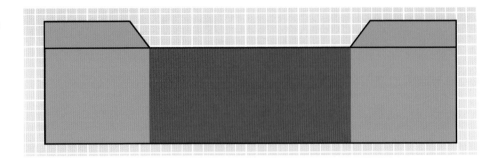

Probably the first major manufacturer of terrain tiles, in the UK at least, was TSS (Total System Scenics). To standardise on the depth of roads and rivers, TSS terrain tiles are composites of two-layers (Figure 34). If you decide to create your own tile terrain system, you should adopt a similar principle to ensure that your terrain panels will match each other.

Terrain tiles can be purchased in a mix of terrain types on a single tile as was the case with *Dieppe 1942* presented by the Loughborough Wargames Club, that combined sea, sand and fields (Figure 35).

Before leaving terrain tiles, another approach is that taken by the Pitsea PAKfront with their modern 1/300th game, *Red Storm Rising*, which used different coloured carpet/floor tiles to create their ground and river terrain as well as the step-contoured hills (Figure 36). Torbay Games Group similarly used carpet for their First World War *Wings of Glory* game (Figure 37).

Figure 35:
*Dieppe 1942.
(The Loughborough
Wargames Club)*

Figure 36:
Red Storm Rising
on carpet tiles.
(*The Pitsea
PAKfront*)

Figure 37:
A Sopwith Snipe
and Albatros DV
fight it out over
carpet terrain.
(*The Torbay Games
Group*)

Hex Terrain

Before leaving the subject of terrain tiles I should mention hex tiles, which wargamers tend to either love or hate.

The thinking behind the hex tile concept is that with six sides as opposed to the four of a square or rectangular terrain tile – there are more exit and entry points per tile, allowing more flexibility in terms of layout. Additionally, some wargamers prefer not to have to bother with measuring distances, or favour rule systems that are based around stylised hex movement. The other area where hex terrain is very popular is amongst wargamers who want to convert one of the many hex-based boardgames into a miniatures game.

Probably the most prolific producer of hex tiles is Kallistra with their Hexon II® system. Hexon II has a wide choice of hex tiles including a particularly impressive trench system as used by Rob Broom for his *Operation Radetsky* game (Figure 38). Hexon II tiles are made from high impact polymer (hard plastic to the rest of us), and are strong but lightweight, easily stackable for storage and feature a unique clip system to ensure that the tiles don't move or separate when in use (Figure 39).

To be perfectly honest, although I really enjoy making terrain for my own use and for customers, there are some things I just can't be bothered to do, one of which is making my own hex tiles. If you like the idea of hex tile terrain, I would recommend that you buy ready-cut tiles, unless you can accurately and consistently cut out numerous hexes (which I can't).

Figure 38:
Operation Radetsky.
(Rob Broom)

Figure 39:
Hexon II clip
system.

Figure 40:
*Battle of Britain
1940.
(The Wessex
Wargamers –
Winchester)*

Having said that, quite a few wargamers buy the basic hex terrain and adapt it to suit their specific requirements. It looks as if the Wessex Wargamers: Winchester even made an attempt to paint the White Cliffs of Dover on the sides of their Hexon II tiles for their game, *Battle of Britain 1940* (Figure 40).

Custom or Sculpted Terrain

We all know that real terrain is seldom flat. An American Civil War game, *The First Battle of Manassas* by the Southend Wargames Club, very effectively recreated the rolling countryside that was a feature of this area of North America (Figure 41). Having first obtained a topographical map of the battlefield, this was overlaid with a Google Earth® aerial photograph and the terrain was then painstakingly sculpted from high density foam panels, which were then textured and flocked to create the final effect. And all in 1/300th scale too.

The recreation of the terrain for *Little Round Top* presented by *Wargames Illustrated* and built by TM Terrain is an example of a finely detailed terrain for a very specific battle but it has limited subsequent gaming options: namely a charge up a hilltop (Figure 42).

When making your own custom terrain, you have the potential to accurately recreate your own representation of historical battlefields, albeit with various adaptations to fit the figure scale. This was the case with the terrain for *The Battle of Alma*, which I built for Crawley Wargames Club and which won a Best Terrain award at Salute (Figure 43).

Figure 41:
*The First Battle of Manassas.
(The Southend Wargames Club)*

Figure 42: *Little Round Top.* (*Wargames Illustrated*)

Storage can often be a major problem with custom terrain, particularly when it incorporates steep hills and slopes. The Bideford and District Wargamers created their club terrain almost like a 3D jigsaw and used it to good effect for their game *One-Armed Sutton* set in China in 1924 (Figure 44).

Figure 43: *Alma*: a 6mm battlefield. (*The Crawley Wargames Club*)

Figure 44:
One-Armed Sutton:
The Great Wall
1924.
(The Bideford and
District Wargamers)

Figure 45:
The aptly named
Austell takes
centre stage.
In *Open Seas –*
Somalia.
(The St. Austell
Wargamers)

For anyone interested, the title of this game related to Frank 'One-Armed' Sutton, who lost part of his wrist at Gallipoli. He was in a trench, throwing back unexploded Turkish grenades, when in his own words, 'I was bound in the course of time to misfield, and I did.' Apparently he found time to retrieve his golf clubs from the beach, after which a surgeon removed the rest of his wrist, and henceforth he was known as 'One-Armed' Sutton. He later took up employment with a Chinese warlord, and invented a primitive armoured vehicle based on a Holt tractor.

And of course sometimes the whole idea of terrain in its own right gets turned on its head, as was the case with *Open Seas: Somalia 2010* by the St Austell Wargamers, in which the most intense gameplay took place on a magnificent scratch-built container ship (Figure 45).

3

Before You Get Started

What is the best type of terrain? There's no universal answer to this question. It depends on many factors including space, cost, time and aesthetics.

For many wargamers, particularly those who wargame at home, the first 'space' consideration is how large a playing area do you want to create? *Isandlwana* by Team Zulu, was most definitely a large game and was created to display the forces involved in this 1879 battle on a one-to-one basis! Fortunately, apart from the famous hill lending its name to the battle, the terrain is relatively multi-use and can be conveniently folded away (Figure 46).

Figure 46:
Isandlwana.
(Team Zulu)

The second consideration is how much space is available for storing the terrain safely when not in use? And there's another space consideration that is often ignored in the enthusiasm to get started: transportation. A good friend of mine constructed a truly impressive medieval fortress on a baseboard a little over 120cm x 60cm, with the towers of the keep over 30cm high once you included the height of the motte. Everything was fine until it came to fitting it into the boot of his relatively small car. It still looked fantastic, but it wouldn't fit in until the rear seats were removed; so when designing your terrain and scenery, try to plan for every eventuality, just in case.

'Cost' is also a factor. How much money are you willing to spend on your terrain? Making your own terrain will usually be cheaper than buying ready-made, but there is still a cost, so it's worth planning out and budgeting what you think you'll need. Always allow a margin though, because invariably you'll miss something off the list. I do it all the time.

As for 'time': do you have the spare time available to make your own terrain, or perhaps more importantly, the time to finish it? There's little more soul destroying than starting a project and being unable to complete it, irrespective of the reason.

Finally: 'aesthetics'. This is a classic grey area. I know it's stating the obvious, but wargaming is a game. Just how important to you are the aesthetics of that game? Are you determined to create a replica of a specific battlefield even though that may limit its use for other conflicts? Or, at the opposite extreme, do you just want a surface upon which to deploy your troops that is more attractive than the dining room table?

To help you consider the options, the following table summarises the most important advantages and disadvantages of the most popular types of terrain.

Terrain type	Advantages	Disadvantages
Terrain cloth	Convenient to transport and store. Light.	Can look bland and uninteresting unless dyed and/or dressed up with scatter material.
Terrain tiles	A lot of terrain options available: easy to create different terrain to suit geographic locations. Light.	Built-in roads and rivers limit set-up options. Some commercially available tiles use easy to damage foam.
Hex tiles	A wide range of terrain options including hills, rivers and trenches. Durable and relatively easy to store.	The formalised hex design can be off putting, and it makes estimating ranges very easy.
Sculpted terrain	Gives the opportunity to accurately recreate specific battlefields.	Can be expensive and time consuming to create, and may offer limited playability for other periods and scenarios.

Future-proofing

My main consideration, once I've finalised the general details and costing of a project, is future-proofing. I want the terrain I make today to match the terrain I make in ten years time, which means creating a series of standards.

Whatever terrain you decide to make, it's a good idea to start a notebook detailing everything to do when creating terrain, such as the materials and paints used. By all means open a file on your computer in which to keep this information. Call me a latter day Luddite, but I never trust solely to digital means to store important information, and I always keep a hard copy.

TERRAIN CLOTH STANDARDS

Given that a basic terrain cloth onto which roads or rivers are laid is the most generic of terrain systems and probably one of the cheapest, future-proofing is easy: just buy as many basic cloths or throws as you think you'll need, even though you may not use them immediately. My throws were approximately 240cm x 200cm and cost just £15 each. I bought three and my terrain cloth future-proofing was solved as I can never envisage needing a maximum playing area bigger than 600cm x 240cm. Bearing in mind that soon after my purchase a colleague from our local wargame club went to buy some more throws from the same store and was told they'd sold out and

Figure 47: Andy Duff's French cavalry prepare to advance over a terrain cloth.

wouldn't be getting any more in, it was a useful lesson … if you can afford it, buy it when you see it because when you want it, it will probably be gone!

The terrain for *A Close Run Thing* by Andy Duff (Figure 47), comprised a basic cloth over which was scattered a mix of materials including gravel, fine shingle and small pebbles, to which hedges and trees were added, in fact everything needed to create a very effective battlefield.

Terrain Tiles and Custom Terrain

There is likely to be slightly more record keeping when it comes to terrain tiles and custom terrain simply because there are far more options. Start by noting down the supplier of the basic high density foam material and any references or code numbers.

The next technique or materials that need to be recorded relate to the texturing of the surface. For example, if making grassy, temperate terrain, I first cover the surface with PVA glue followed by a sprinkling of sand. Although a variation in texture is fine, I prefer not to see such a variation running obviously along the edge of a terrain panel. Fortunately sand is not particularly expensive. I bought a large sack of it, and after several years of use, the sack is still a little over half full.

After the sand coating I paint the surface using a sequence of Dulux® colours – which have the advantages of being far more economical than using model paints – and they have a precise naming and referencing system,

Figure 48:
These 15mm Essex Miniatures 'Death or Glory boys' are having a bit of trouble with this terrain designed for larger scale figures.

either of which can be quoted and the exact colour can be recreated … now that really is future-proofing.

For my temperate terrain panels I apply a dark brown undercoat followed by a drybrush of mid brown, finished off with a very light drybrush of pale yellow. To simulate grass I use autumn static grass because the green is less lurid than many of the summer static grass products available.

If you are making an arid desert-like terrain, you might want to include some gravel or similar material on the surface to make the terrain appear more rugged. Bear in mind that the larger the grains the more difficult it will be for figures, vehicles or even buildings to stand flat on the terrain (Figure 48). In my experience it's best to use a material that is coarse enough to be drybrushed but still fine enough to place figures or buildings on easily. You can always add loose gravel or lichen to add more interest to the terrain. As with the temperate terrain panels, keep a note of the paints used so that you can create and match in more panels if required at a later date.

Terrain Cloths

4

For my land-based terrain cloths I use a throw because I like the way that most of them are double-sided with one surface having a short pile, the other a longer one, so you can simulate different lengths of grass.

Throws are available in a wide range of colours, but unsurprisingly, the most useful are the green and sometimes brown ones. As manufactured, the single colour can be rather bland and uninteresting, so I spray my throws with yellow, brown and green; my technique is to hang the throw from a washing line and then spray it, keeping the effect as subtle as possible. I always try to spray outside, but even so I recommend wearing a suitable mask, because otherwise a sudden gust of wind can easily give you a mouth or nose full of spray paint: which isn't ideal to put it mildly. If you have a spray gun or airbrush you can mix up your own colours to suit your particular needs, but keep a record of the mix in case you want to create more terrain cloths that need to match. Although they work out more expensive, future-proofing of colours is much easier if you use aerosols; just keep a note of the brand and colours used.

Another colouring option is to dye the cloth. I tend to avoid this method because it can take ages for a thick throw to dry and I'm always working against the clock, but you can get some interesting effects if you're patient.

As far as the basic terrain cloth is concerned, that's about it. The easiest way to simulate hills is to adopt the approach used in the early days of wargaming: slide a suitable object under the cloth. I have several hills that I made years ago from polystyrene packaging that are too easily damaged to be used on their own but are perfectly acceptable when placed beneath a terrain cloth. When thinking about the hills that you'll be placing underneath your terrain cloth, bear in mind that probably the main reason that you've opted for terrain cloth terrain is to reduce the amount of storage space needed. If you make your hills too large, you risk the hills taking up more space than the cloth, so if you feel that you need large hills, make them in small sections which are easier to store and less likely to get accidentally damaged. With the basic topography for your battle sorted out, the next stage is to think about adding rivers and roads.

Rivers are undeniably a problem if you're using a terrain cloth, and their appearance on the terrain cloth requires a measure of compromise. Water features look better if they are set below the level of the surrounding ground, by raising the cloth with carefully cut panels or blocks underneath to create the river banks and then running blue felt or similar material between the banks to form the river. The problem is that by the time you've created the under-terrain you've effectively negated the main benefit of the cloth-based terrain system, namely that it doesn't take up much space. In fact, if you're going to make a complete supporting terrain over which to drape your cloth, why are you bothering with the cloth, why not just make or use terrain panels? Anyway, it's worth thinking about.

However, if you're determined to incorporate rivers into your terrain cloth but you don't want to build a supporting system beneath, there are several other options depending on the material being used. If you're using fleece, you can simply paint on your rivers and perhaps line the river banks with pebbles. If you're using a fur throw, the best option is to carefully shave off the fur and then paint the exposed areas accordingly. Neither option is ideal in my opinion because the underlying texture of both materials is very unlike water. My preference would be to either make your own separate river sections as shown in Chapter Seven, or use special river pieces such as those marketed by Gale Force Nine in their Battlefield in a Box range (Figure 49).

Integrating roads into cloth terrain creates fewer problems than rivers. You can paint them directly onto the throw, but a better option is to shave away the fur and then paint onto the exposed material (Figure 50). An alternative approach is to spread flexible sealer onto the shaved areas, give this a brown basecoat and then lightly drybrush to bring out the texture, as was the case with this *War of the Spanish Succession* game by SEEMS (Figure 51). You can miss out the brown basecoat stage if you use brown sealant.

Figure 49:
A river section by Gale Force Nine.

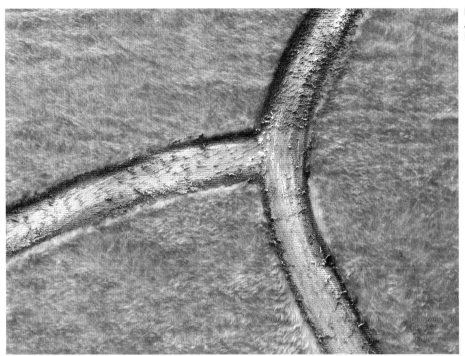

Figure 50:
A road integrated into a throw.

Figure 51:
A road made by spreading flexible sealer into a shaved throw.

Figure 52:
An enhanced cloth terrain with a mix of materials.
(*The St Austell Wargamers*)

With your main terrain features either cut into the terrain or lying on top, you can enhance the appearance further by sprinkling around some other materials such as lichen, dried moss or sponge, as was well demonstrated in *Alien versus Predator* by the St. Austell Wargamers. This game showcased another useful source of foliage: the plastic plants sold in pet shops to decorate aquariums (Figure 52).

Just remember that all the foliage and loose detail added to your terrain will have to be collected up at the end of your game, and unless you're really patient you'll never be able to separate it, so eventually you will finish up with a container full of very mixed scatter material.

Desert (Arid) Terrain

For desert terrain cloths you need a base material that you can spray if you wish to break up the single colour, and onto which you can add suitable loose scatter material (Figure 53). In my experience, the best material as the basis for a desert terrain cloth is fleece, because it doesn't crease.

Another material used for a desert terrain cloth is blown vinyl wallpaper that, like fleece, can look very effective when covered with scatter material and scenery as demonstrated in *Hammers Slammers* presented by the Wessex Wyverns (Figure 54).

Figure 53:
Carry on up the Levant.
(*The South East Essex Military Society*)

Figure 54:
Hammers Slammers game on blown vinyl wallpaper.
(*The Wessex Wyverns*)

Snow Terrain

Snow terrain is slightly different from the other two types of terrain, depending on whether you are looking for a light sprinkling of snow or a dense snow covered landscape. (Figure 55)

If the former, the best option is to sprinkle suitable material over a green terrain cloth after you've positioned all the terrain, scenery and buildings. As for which material to use, on this occasion, cheap is best and I have used virtually anything I could put my hands on including sugar, salt and even baking powder. The biggest problem is getting a reasonable covering to stay on your trees and buildings because unless you apply some form of glue, the snow just slides off. One option is to spray photo mount or even hair lacquer onto your scenery, but if you do, it's probable that you'll be stuck with those particular scenery items being only useful for snow scenes for the foreseeable future. Another consideration with loose snow is that as you move your troops around you'll finish up displacing the snow, which can look rather odd.

For reproducing dense snow, I use a piece of white fleece. As usual the expanse of a single colour can be improved by being broken up a little. If you look at paintings or photographs of snow, the shadow areas often have a slightly blue tinge, so I very lightly spray patches of pale blue onto the white fleece. As with the light sprinkling of snow, once you've positioned your scenery and buildings, sprinkle some snow over them to blend them in.

Figure 55:
A battery of 10mm Pendraken French Napoleonic artillery weather the storm.

Sea Terrain

This is probably the easiest terrain cloth to make. You can simply use a piece of blue fleece and that's it. I know that apart from the Aegean on a good day, and the Caribbean most of the time, the sea isn't a pure blue, but for the purposes of wargaming it will do. If you can find it, a blue-grey fleece is probably more representative of the North Atlantic, but whatever colour you choose you can always give it subtle sprays of green or grey to tone it down. How much work you put in is up to you (Figure 56). If your sea battles are going to take place close to land, sprinkle fine sand along the edge of the land masses to represent sandy beaches. I'd probably draw the line at beach towels and wind-breaks though.

Another material that I use for simulating sea terrain is a large photographic backdrop that I no longer use for its original purpose. It's a mottled mix of greens, dark blues and grey, and works very well. It's also 300cm x 180cm, so no shortage of sea for even relatively large fleet actions.

Before leaving the sea cloth concept, I thought I'd mention the *Raid of Le Vengeur* presented by the Society of Fantasy and Science Fiction Wargamers (SFSFW) as an interesting solution to the problem of making a naval game – albeit in a fantasy environment – into three dimensions to accommodate surface vessels and submarines (Figure 57). As long-suffering colleagues in

Figure 56:
Sea terrain mat and island.

Figure 57:
A novel way
of combining
underwater and
surface combat.
(*The Society of
Fantasy and Science
Fiction Wargamers*)

my local wargame club will be only too well aware, I've been playing around with the idea of creating a Second World War North Atlantic convoy game for ages. Perhaps there's something in this SFSFW game that could be adapted?

TERRAIN TILES

5

Terrain tiles were probably one of the first major innovations in wargame terrain, and they continue to be very popular. They are relatively easy to store, offer considerable flexibility when it comes to creating different battlefield layouts, and if you buy or make ones that use the best quality materials, they'll last for ages.

As with any terrain design, the first decision you have to make is whether you intend to create roads or rivers as integral parts of your terrain panels or if will you be using separate components? If the former, I recommend that you ensure that your terrain is designed in such a way as to make it easy to add river tiles at a later date. The simplest way to achieve this, and also ensure that the height of your ground and water levels always match up, is to adopt a lamination approach where the lower tile is 3cm in depth and creates the water level, and the ground is made from a thinner layer of 1cm thick material on top of this (Figure 58). In effect, all your terrain tiles start as water level tiles onto which you glue the land. Not only must the depth of your terrain tiles be standardised but so too must the entry and exit points for terrain features, like roads and river that spread across the terrain panels. To ensure maximum flexibility when configuring different terrain layouts these features should enter and leave the panels at their centre point.

If you intend to use separate roads and rivers and just lay them on top of your terrain tiles, it doesn't matter how or where they feature on your plan. However I'm assuming that you want to create a collection of tiles with the integrated terrain features. With that in mind, next decide on your playing area and then on the size of your individual terrain tiles. Generally the most commonly seen size for terrain panels is 60cm x 60cm x 40cm, and coincidently this size of raw high density foam block is readily available, so

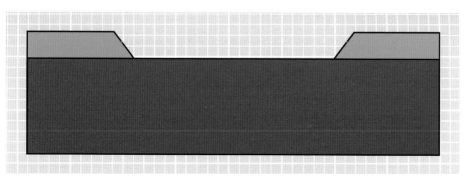

Figure 58:
Lamination terrain cross section.

49

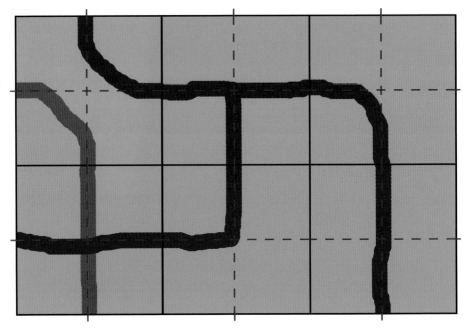

Figure 59:
A suggested terrain layout showing how roads and rivers enter and leave at the centre of each tile edge.

if your can store tiles of this dimension, I suggest that you adopt it. Draw a scale grid to represent your tiled playing area. It helps to also mark the centre lines for each tile.

With your playing area determined, the next stage is to plan out the actual terrain. Don't be too adventurous to begin with, and remember that although rivers add visual interest to your terrain, they can also restrict gameplay by creating choke points which channel movement and usually result in a lot of battles being fought over bridges, which can get a bit tedious. Remember too, that your roads and rivers should enter and leave terrain tiles at the centre points along edges of your panels (Figure 59).

Once you have finalised your plan you need to buy your basic tiles. I suggest that you only buy tiles that are already cut to size. It is possible to cut your own tiles from sheet material but I've never been very successful at doing so and wouldn't recommend it. There are quite a few companies who sell various brands of high density foam under their own brand names. High density foam intended for heat insulation purposes tends to be sold in a standard thickness of 6cm deep. However the Styrofoam and Craftfoam brands are generally marketed in thicknesses from 0.3cm up to 15cm. You'll often find it marketed as pink, blue or green high density foam just to confuse matters. Always buy the densest material that you can afford because the stronger it is, the more likely it will withstand regular storage, transportation and wargame usage. This is a very important consideration. The wargames club to which I now belong purchased a large quantity of terrain tiles and despite them being stored carefully in boxes, after a relatively short time, the edges got chipped, and thumb and elbow dents in the playing surface started to dictate where trees and buildings had to be placed to conceal them.

If you only want a small number of panels it's easy enough to find retailers who sell a wide range of high density foam materials, but for larger quantities it's usually more cost-effective to purchase direct from manufacturers, and you'll be surprised how many panels you'll use once you get started. Even if you can't find a use for all the tiles it's more than likely that there will be other wargamers in your group who'll take any overs off your hands ... for a price of course.

Integrated Rivers

So now, assuming that you're following the suggested cross section already shown, take your river panels and mark the position of the banks. Carefully cut out the river sections. River banks look better if they are sloping (Figure 60), but it is easier to cut them with vertical edges and then chamfer the angle afterwards.

It's important that the width of your rivers and the profile of the river banks are the same where they enter and leave a terrain tile so that they match up properly, but they can vary during their journey from one edge of the tile to another, and in my opinion they look more interesting that way too.

Figure 60:
TSS River terrain tile.

At this stage, glue together your water and land sections. Weight them down and leave them at least 48 hours so that the glue dries thoroughly.

To create the river surface, I paint the river bed with Smooth Ripple texture paint. Texture paint contains a plasticiser that helps the paint retain the texture given to it when using a sponge paint roller. Smooth Ripple gives quite a subtle texture, but if you're trying to simulate a fast moving river you can drag a small paintbrush along the painted surface and following the general line of the river bank.

The flowing river effect can be further enhanced by brushing undiluted PVA glue onto the surface, dragging a brush through the glue when it's almost dry. PVA glue settles as it dries, so if you use this technique you'll probably need to apply several layers until you're satisfied with the end result. I have also seen this technique used as a substitute for using the textured paint.

Integrated Roads

If you want to make separate roads, see Chapter Fifteen. For integrated rural-type roads, I first slightly recess them into the surface of the high density foam using a Stanley Surform block plane (Figure 61). Next I fill the road recess with paintable, flexible brown sealant, and before it dries I use a section of old broken comb (I told you I never throw anything away), to scratch ruts into the road surface. The road is then given a light drybrush of sandy yellow to simulate a light coating of dust and to pick out the tops of the ruts (Figure 62). The surrounding terrain is then painted and tufts or static grass can be applied along the verges (Figure 63). If the road or track only has light or relatively infrequent traffic, I might also glue some static grass along the centre line. Depending on the location of the road, it can further be enhanced by painting dark brown or black into the ruts and then given them a coat of gloss varnish to suggest water.

For tarmac roads I adopt a very different approach. The road is made using use wet-and-dry paper or belt sander refills. The main difference between these materials is that wet-and-dry is available in sheet form (usually around A4 sized), whereas the belt sander refills can be found in widths from 1cm to 15cm and in lengths from 53cm to 122cm. Both these materials are available in different grades: the lower the number (such as 40 or 60) the coarser the surface. The smaller the scale of figures or vehicles that will be using your tarmac roads, the finer the grade of material should be.

Once you have decided on the width and shape of your roads, it's just a matter of cutting them out and fixing them into place on your terrain panels. Conventional PVA glue doesn't work well with wet-and-dry: in my experience the material curls as soon as you apply the PVA. It's basically not sticky quickly enough, so I use double-sided industrial tape designed to hold carpet underlay and floor tiles in place. To help seal the wet-and-dry to the terrain panel, when I add the texture to the ground surrounding the road, I

Figure 61:
Recessing a road using a block plane.

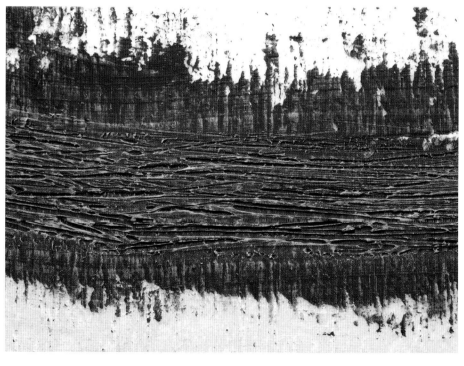

Figure 62:
A rural road showing the rutted surface.

Figure 63:
A close-up of a completed section of rural road.

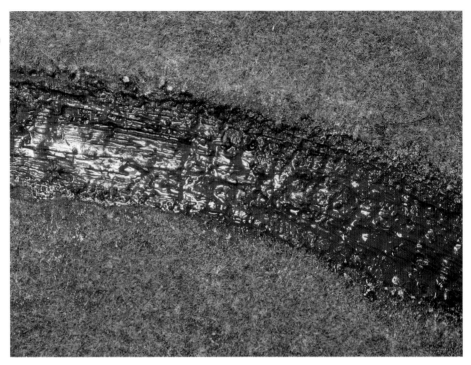

Figure 64:
A finished section of tarmac road.

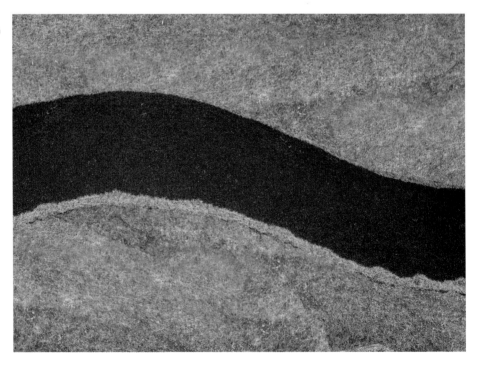

slightly overlap the edges with PVA glue, so that the texture material helps bond the wet-and-dry in position. For painting the tarmac road, wet-and-dry paper is generally black, so you can leave it as it is; however sanding belts are available in different colours, so they will probably have to be painted black or dark grey (Figure 64). Wet-and-dry paper and sanding belts can also be used to create separate roads, by fixing them onto a suitable base material such as self-adhesive vinyl floor tiles to prevent them curling.

Desert Terrain Tiles

My technique for creating desert tiles developed from one of life's fortunate accidents, but more of that in a moment. Referring back to the creation of temperate zone terrain tiles, although it's unlikely that your desert tiles will need too much in the way of flowing rivers (unless you're restaging the Nile River War or something similar), you may still have a use for dried river beds, so create your tiles in the same basic way. However, instead of applying a coat of smooth ripple textured paint to the river area, treat the river bed in the same way as the surrounding area, possibly with a few large boulders added for effect.

But back to how I created the main desert surface. I was making some desert terrain panels for a customer, and I was in a hurry, which is never conducive to creating your best work.

My first step was to give the surface of my tiles a thick coating of PVA glue onto which I sprinkled a mixture of fine sand, aquarium gravel and small pebbles. It was at that point I sowed the seeds for my potential disaster: although I'd set the terrain panels aside to allow the PVA glue to dry overnight, my overnight was rather short because I'd been working on them until 3am! In the morning I checked the surface of the tiles and the surface appeared to be dry, so I applied a coat of pale yellow emulsion paint and left the tiles to dry again while I got on with another commission. When I checked the tiles again 24 hours later, the paint was still damp, so I resorted to most modelmakers' and painters' stand-by: a hairdryer. The tiles were given a thorough blast of hot air and set aside again. Later that day I checked the surface again to find that it was completely dry ... note that I said, the surface! When I returned to the tiles several days later prior to packing them up for despatch I discovered a very interesting and unexpected result: I think what happened was that my application of the hairdryer had dried the top surface of the paint, but the PVA glue was still drying out, and as it did so it pulled the paint surface causing it to crack. I think that the end result worked out rather well, albeit unpredictably, and certainly the customer was very pleased at what he clearly thought was a very clever and deliberate technique on my part (Figure 65). Of course when he reads this book, he'll know the truth.

Sea Terrain Panels

I use a sea terrain mat or photographic background most of the time, but I have occasionally been asked to make sea terrain panels for customers, and I always keep records of the technique and material ready for future orders. In my experience, unless you create your sea texture and paint the panels at the same time, it's very difficult to match them, particularly if you try to create a mottled blue/green look. So I would always urge anyone making sea terrain panels to try to make them all at the same time.

Another consideration is the waves; what might be just a gentle swell for a 1:2400th scale First World War dreadnought could be a raging gale for a similar model in 1:6000th scale.

I use a smooth ripple texture paint to create a subtle texture. Another reason for keeping a record of how you create the surface of the sea, and the colours used, is to ensure that your bases will blend in with the sea. Bear in mind that whenever you use white textured paint or filler you should always consider adding paint to the mix to reduce the risk of any white showing through if the panel gets damaged. The mixing-in process lightens the base material, so use as dark a colour as possible. Ideally use powder paints because they won't thin the textured paint or the filler; there isn't a particularly wide choice of powder paints, so if in doubt, just use black.

Figure 66:
Basic sea terrain
in use comparing
a GHQ 1/2400th
Iron Duke with a
1/6000th vessel by
Hallmark.

When it comes to actually creating the sea, you can either give the surface a basecoat of very dark blue and then overpaint it with a mottling of lighter blues and greens, or simply use a single colour (Figure 66). Once you're satisfied with the look of the sea, you can give it a coat of varnish. The temptation is to use gloss, but I prefer the more subtle effect of a satin varnish. Finally, once the varnish has thoroughly dried, add white highlights to the wave tops, but don't overdo it.

Snow Terrain Panels

I must be honest, I have always steered clear of making snow terrain. Not because it's particularly difficult to make; it's no more complicated than any other terrain, but more because unless I was planning to wargame Napoleon's invasion of Russia in 1812, or a similar campaign, I just never felt that I would get enough use out of the terrain to justify my work. However if you are determined to create your own snow terrain panels you could do a lot worse than follow the example set by Crawley Wargames Club with their game *Fraustadt 1706* (Figure 67). First, the gently rolling terrain of the battlefield was made by cutting and sanding foam panels to shape. The areas which were to represent exposed expanses of frozen water were painted with a dark green/blue mix and given a coat of gloss varnish. The remaining areas of the terrain were painted a combination of brown and green, and in places where the impression of very deep snow was to be represented, pure

Figure 67:
A battle in the snow. (*Freustadt* by *The Crawley Wargames Club*)

Figure 68:
A close-up of frozen water terrain.

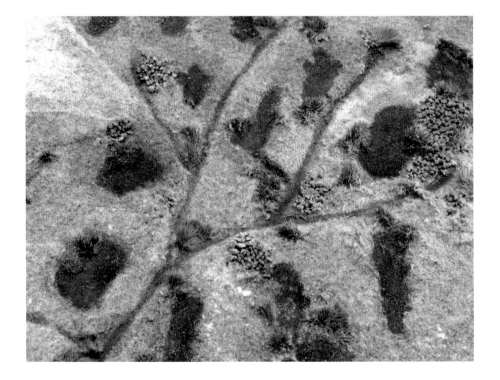

white was used. Next, working in small sections at a time, the terrain was given a coating of PVA glue onto which was sprinkled static grass 'snow'. Finally exposed tufts of grass and stones were glued in place (Figure 68).

Another snow terrain game was *Winter War* by Baker Company (Figure 69). The basic terrain comprised mdf panels that had foam sheet glued on top, onto and into which the foxholes added. All the panels were coated with plaster, which was then given a random coating of PVA glue and fine sand, and finally the panels were painted white and grey.

Did the Earth Move for You?

Having made your terrain tiles, there's one problem of which you should be aware. Unless you do something to prevent it, they can easily be knocked or moved which can result, at best, in a narrow gap between panels and at worst a veritable chasm into which may plummet your elite forces ... which is guaranteed to destroy even the best thought out strategies (Figure 70).

I've tried various options. One of the most successful and simplest has been to staple strips of sandpaper to the underside of each panel. A piece of cheap cloth or fleece is then spread over the surface on which the game is to be played. The terrain panels are then positioned on the cloth and the sandpaper grips the surface of the fleece. Cheap and cheerful: but it works.

Another solution to the 'earth moving' problem with terrain tiles is that adopted by Levellers Wargames Club, Weymouth and the Weymouth

Figure 70:
Terrain tile tectonic
plate movement?

Figure 71:
Arracourt:
September 1944.
(*The Levellers*
Wargames Club
and Weymouth
Warlords)

Figure 72:
A terrain panel enclosing frame system.

Figure 73:
Attention to detail that makes all the difference.

Warlords for their *Arracourt: September 1944* game (Figure 71). They created a wooden framework to enclose the tiles, which was held together using bolts and wing nuts … simple but effective (Figure 72).

Taking the idea of a frame a little further, the Brixham Berserkers built the terrain for their *Valhalla* game onto two boards, each of which were edged with skirting board which was then stained and varnished to create a truly professional job. The two boards clamped securely together for an immovable playing area, and the added detail of the intricate designs at each corner was the sort of attention to detail that I really like to see (Figure 73).

Another solution to the dreaded moving terrain is to build the entire terrain into a single box. The Pike and Shot Society came up with a novel idea for their 15mm *Second Battle of Newbury* game (Figure 74). They took a conventional pasting table, separated the two halves, turned them upside down, and then re-fixed them side-by-side to create a more usable playing area that neatly unfolded for gaming and could be folded away in seconds when the battle was won (or lost).

Figure 74:
The Royalist forces about to take another 'pasting' at Newbury.
(*The Pike and Shot Society*)

Custom or Sculpted Terrain

6

I suppose that the first question must be, 'What's the difference between terrain tiles and custom or sculpted terrain?' I think that there are several answers:

- Custom or sculpted terrain has as much as possible integrated into the terrain.
- Roads, rivers, hills, even walls, are all built in.
- Custom terrain is still usually based around panels but generally they are larger than what many wargamers consider to be the standard: 60cm x 60cm.

Probably the most significant difference however, is that terrain cloths and tiles are intended to be as multi-purpose as possible, with the most important features of your chosen battle being added as individual components. By contrast, custom terrain is usually designed and built for a specific battle that may seriously limit the subsequent usefulness of the terrain. It is for this reason that many custom terrain set-ups are created as demonstration or participation games for wargame shows.

A particularly impressive example of this type of terrain was *Corunna 1809* created by the Essex Gamesters (Robert Browning and Ron Ringrose), which was more like a military museum exhibit than a wargame table (Figures 75–76). But what wargamer worth his salt wouldn't relish the opportunity to take part in a game on terrain that combines both land and sea battles to the same scale and on the same terrain set up?

Just how much scenery is built as a part of the basic terrain varies, but it's usual for roads, rivers and even walls to be integrated. Sometimes custom terrain may have limited uses for other battles because it's just too specific, but its reusability can depend on how the terrain was initially designed. For example, *Gelderland 1945* created by the Sussex Massif features flooded terrain with a few isolated areas of relatively high ground and several partially submerged houses with the roofs poking above the water level (Figure 77). This is not the sort of custom terrain which on first glance could easily be used in other scenarios perhaps, but since the base making up the flooded terrain is separate from the islands, it could be used for other primarily water themed games, perhaps a brown water Vietnam naval game in the Mekong Delta … and the buildings can stand in for almost any Northern European Second World War game.

Figure 75:
Corunna 1809.
(*The Essex Gamesters*)

Figure 76:
British troops await the French attack outside Corunna.

Figure 77:
Gelderland 1945.
(The Sussex Massif)

PROJECT 1: A Harbour and Canals

This special project is one that I undertook for the Minehead Wargames Club (Figure 78). Originally it was intended for use with buildings, figures and a game system, produced by a well-known wargame manufacturer, but since they advised that they would sue me if I featured photographs of any of their products or named any of their games in this book, some details have been changed! This actually worked out better all round because the terrain proved to be usable across a much broader historical period, from early medieval to the Second World War and – of course – fantasy.

MATERIALS
* 0.5cm thick high density foam
* Textured vinyl wallpaper
* Balsa and cocktail sticks
* Map pins
* Wet-and-dry paper
* Thick card

CONSTRUCTION

As with any large project, the first step was planning, and so I drew up a layout that I felt would offer some challenging gameplay within the relatively limited area allocated to the game (Figure 79). The red lines show the 60cm squares, the dark blue the water and the area in the bottom right corner represents a section of the harbour.

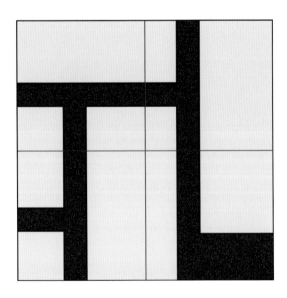

One lesson I learned early in my terrain-making life was to check if the customer intended to use a particular set of rules because these can influence some aspects of the terrain. For example, if the rules specify that a figure can jump down or climb up a certain distance without any movement penalty, then that needs to be borne in mind when planning the model. Similarly the distance that a figure can safely jump can influence the width of any gaps: in this case the width of the canals.

The construction technique was the same for each of the four terrain pieces, so I'll only show the construction process for one of the terrain modules.

I started by cutting out a series of high density foam strips 4.5cm high, which with the 0.5cm panel that would be placed on top, would result in a canal and harbour wall that was 5cm high. Supports were added to the wall sections to keep them perpendicular during gluing, to make the box section sturdier and also provide additional support for the upper panel (Figure 80).

I use anything I can when trying to make a right angle. In this case, as well as the ubiquitous Lego bricks, I used a couple of right angle bracing pieces, and then glued this first wall section to a 60cm x 60cm piece of high density foam (Figure 81).

I then glued one adjacent wall to the first one (Figure 82). I frequently use pins to hold the components in place while the glue is setting. The remaining walls were then glued into position to create what was in effect, an open-topped box (Figure 83).

Figure 80:
The walls need inner supports.

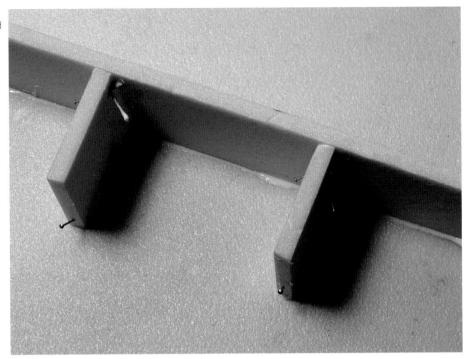

Figure 83:
The remaining walls pinned and glued.

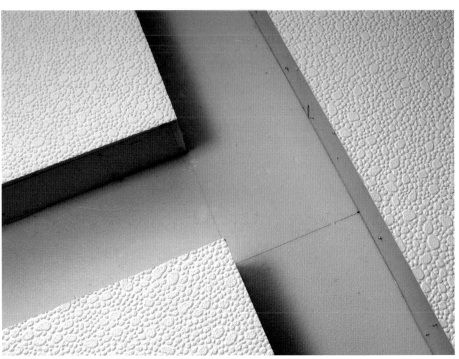

Figure 84:
Modules with textured wallpaper.

I'm never mean when it comes to using glue, at least where it doesn't show. To complete this box section, I cut a piece of high density foam to form a lid. Using this as a template, I next cut a piece of textured wallpaper to the same size, and then pinned and glued the lid in place.

Once the glue had set thoroughly, I glued the textured wallpaper to the lid (Figure 84). The remaining boxes for this particular terrain piece were then assembled and glued in place following the same process.

It's important that you give the wallpaper a thorough and even coating of glue to avoid air bubbles. If you do have problems with air bubbles, make a small cut in the bubble, carefully squeeze some PVA glue into the hole and press the paper down firmly. Don't worry about any partially visible cuts because you can always conceal them with a strategically placed barrel or some rubble.

Next stage is the water, which I created by painting on Smooth Ripple textured paint, then stippling it to break up the surface (Figure 85).

The textured paint was left to dry thoroughly. There are several other ways to simulate water, one of which is to paint the surface in the appropriate colour, and then give it several coats of gloss varnish. When the varnish is completely dry, brush on PVA glue and then stipple it to create waves or ripples. You'll probably have to repeat this latter step, because PVA tends to level itself out. PVA dries almost transparent so that the gloss varnish and the paint are visible through it. Always run tests though when using high

Figure 85:
Water given the rippled texture paint treatment.

Figure 86:
Quay walls with textured wallpaper.

Figure 87:
Slabs edging the quayside.

density foam because solvents or even varnish can react badly with it, and you really don't want to put your painstakingly created terrain at risk.

Once the textured paint had dried, I cut 5cm wide strips of textured wallpaper and glued them to the side walls (Figure 86). My reason for adding these after applying the textured paint was to avoid obscuring the cobbled effect if I was a bit over-enthusiastic with the texturing.

To break up the cobbled surface I added some stone edging made from small pieces of sandpaper. My idea was that the texture of the sandpaper would, when painted and drybrushed, result in a gritty stone slab effect (Figure 87). Unfortunately, and unsurprisingly really since sandpaper isn't supposed to get wet, when I painted the sandpaper square it lifted off all the grit, leaving the paper backing. Next time I'll use wet and dry paper: that doesn't fall apart when it gets wet. The clue was in the name really!

I started painting the cobbled surface black, then drybrushed it grey, which was followed with successively lighter coats of grey to pick out the cobble details (Figure 88). I decided that I wanted a dark look to my water: the sort of water in which you wouldn't willingly choose to take a dip in, but stopped short of the making it look like a sewage outflow. I painted it with a mix of black and dark blue (Figure 89).

With all these waterways and canals, inevitably I was going to need a few bridges. I decided on several options: stone ones with and without parapets and some timber ones too. When constructing bridges you need to bear in

Figure 88: Stonework undercoated in black and after initial grey drybrush.

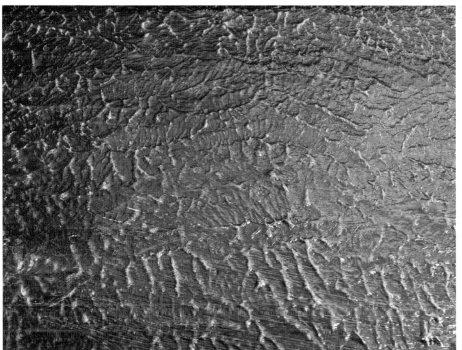

mind the widest width of anything that you might want to be able to pass over the bridge.

I was very careful when constructing my modules to ensure that the waterways were all the same width so that my bridges could fit almost anywhere for maximum set-up options. The construction of suitable wooden bridges is covered in Chapter Sixteen, but for a bit of variety I also made a couple of simple stone bridges.

From high density foam, I cut out two bridge sides to fit the width of my waterways incorporating a curved arch. I could have papered them with textured wallpaper, but decided instead to engrave some random stonework onto the outer surfaces using an old ballpoint pen (Figure 90).

The road surface of this bridge was to be flush with the cobbled quayside, so I deducted the thickness of my high density foam from the total height of the bridge to give me the height of its inner supports; the width was determined by the width of a coach that needed to be able to pass over the bridge without its wheels hanging over the edges. I incorporated four supports for the road, one at each end and one either side of the arch (Figure 91). The basic roadway was cut from 0.5cm high density foam and glued in position (Figure 92). Textured wallpaper was then glued in place to form the roadway (Figure 93).

Figure 90:
The stone bridge
sides.

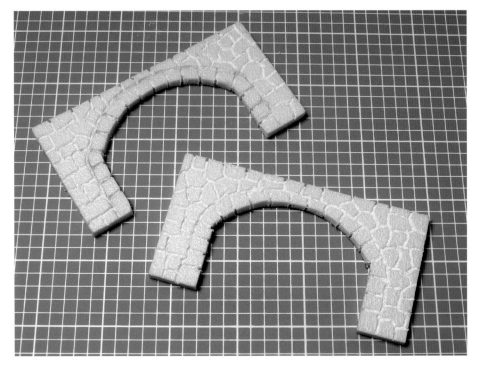

Figure 91:
The bridge
showing the inner
supports.

Figure 92:
The roadway
added.

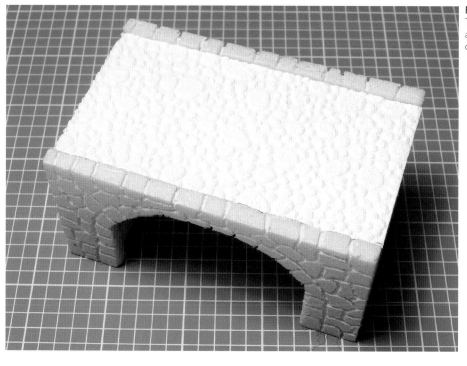

Figure 93:
Textured wallpaper
added to create
cobbled surface.

Figure 94:
Variation of
the bridge
incorporating a
parapet.

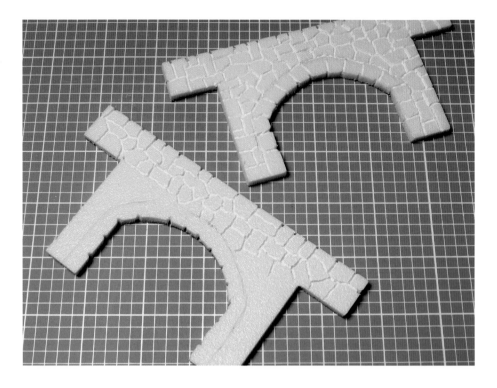

Figure 95:
A bridge in place.

To complete this bridge I cut a length of thin card to form an inner arch. For a bit of variation you can create a bridge with a parapet (Figure 94): it's just a case of making the sides higher and allowing for an overlap of the side walls onto the quayside.

As mentioned at the start of this section, I also made some wooden bridges to go with this terrain project, and the construction for these is explained Chapter Sixteen. Both the stone and wooden bridges followed a similar painting sequence. The models were first painted in grey (I used Dulux Flint), and then they were given a drybrush treatment with successively lighter coats until the required effect was achieved (Figure 95).

I decided that my canals and harbour section would benefit from having some bollards at which ships could be moored. I could have bought them, but I decided to make my own using map pins from my local stationers and some thick card. I cut off all but a short stub of the pin, and glued the pin to a square of card. The resulting item was then sprayed black, and there you have some freestanding bollards (Figure 96).

Of course there are countless other details you can add to give your terrain more interest without making it period or geographically specific. A few upright timbers made from balsa with metal rings added became mooring posts (Figure 97).

To add a bit of variation to the walls, I carefully cut an arch out from one wall section prior to assembly to represent a culvert or possibly a sewer.

Figure 96:
Bollards and yet more bollards.

Figure 97:
Simple mooring
posts.

Figure 98:
The culvert
opening.

Pieces of thin card were cut and glued around the arch and cocktail sticks added to represent the bars (Figure 98).

This terrain project proved extremely popular and was used in many historical and fantasy games with equal success, and I suspect that it will have a long and useful life … which is the best one can expect from one's terrain.

PROJECT 2: *First World War Terrain for* Wings of Glory

When *Wings of Glory* was released it was a little like Christmas and birthday both rolled into one. I've always been fascinated by First World War aircraft, and I vividly remember the ceiling of my childhood bedroom being crisscrossed with nylon fishing line from which were hung various 1/72nd aircraft. Everything was fine until Airfix released their Handley Page 0/400; a magnificent model, but far too heavy for my delicate tracery of fine nylon filament. It was not a great day when I returned home from school to find my squadrons and jastas had plummeted earthwards. Even the ones that had taken a relatively soft landing on my bed were in bits; as was I.

But I digress. *Wings of Glory* with its easy to understand, but necessarily abstracted, rules together with the assembled and ready painted aircraft reignited my interest in the knights of the air, but I quickly realised that a plain green cloth wasn't exactly enhancing my gaming experience and I decided to create some suitable terrain (Figure 99).

Figure 99:
The Red Baron about to bounce an unsuspecting RE8..

MATERIALS

- High density foam panels
- Clump foliage

CONSTRUCTION

Unsurprisingly, when viewed from the air, everything on the ground appears smaller. The *Wings of Glory* First World War models are 1/144th scale, but to enable me to source some useful ground-based items I decided to assume a ground scale of 1/300th, which would make available many excellent models and figures if required, such as those manufactured by Heroics and Ros.

The first stage was to plan out my terrain. I decided to include a suggestion of the two trench frontlines, and then just add some of the area behind to allow space for airfields, towns and even artillery positions as the game expanded.

This project was primarily a painting one, as the only real sculpting was the cutting of the trenches because the terrain needs to be flat so that the bases of the aircraft won't topple over.

The trench networks were cut using my trusty pyrography tool (Figure 100). The wire was bent to create a suitable profile. You need to experiment when setting the temperature. Too low and it won't cut, but too hot and the foam will roll back away from the wire and you won't get vertical edges to your trenches.

Figure 100:
Cutting a trench.

With the trench network cut, the next step is to create the bomb craters that punctuated the desolate No Mans' Land. To form the craters in the surface of the foam I used two readily available and – most importantly – cheap, tools: fingers, thumbs and for larger craters an elbow comes in useful … not exactly high tech, but it works (Figure 101)!

With the trenches and craters created, the next step was to paint the terrain. At this scale this is a relatively abstracted process. Usually I apply texture to my terrain surface, but ultimately I intended to use 1/300th scale troops, AFVs and vehicles on the terrain (Figures 102–103), and I decided that even subtle texture would, at this scale, be to coarse and I'd finish up with troops and vehicles at ungainly angles.

I gave all the panels a black undercoat, and then randomly drybrushed different colours over the panels until I was satisfied with the general appearance. I used mainly Dulux Exotic Spice 2, and Dulux Golden Umber 3, but it's really a case of experimentation. Once the paint dried, I repainted the crater/shell holes with a thinned matt black. I left the panels overnight and carefully painted semi-gloss varnish into the craters to suggest water.

I also wanted to represent the area behind the lines, if only so that I could have some airfields. It was important to delineate the roads without causing problems for the *Wings of Glory* aircraft stands, so I selectively glued clump foliage along the edges of roads. I also sprinkled different colours of flock and scatter material onto the terrain to break up the areas.

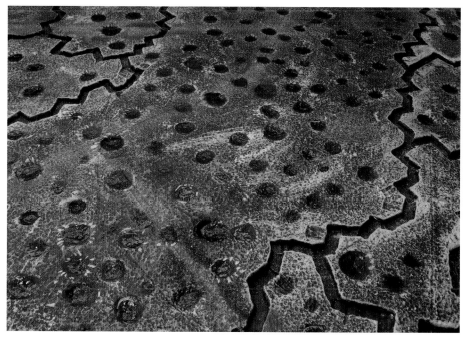

Figure 101:
Painted digit- and elbow-created terrain.

Figure 102:
Heroics and
Ros A7V tanks
suddenly appear in
No Mans' Land.

Figure 103:
A pair of Old Bill
buses on their way
to collect more
troops for the
front line.

Rivers and Ponds

7

W ater features have a major modelmaking advantage over roads: they don't have major changes in level or have to negotiate hills, unless you're modelling the Nile cataracts or something similar.

PROJECT 3: A Simple River Section

MATERIALS

The material used for your river depends on how much effort you want to put in, which in turn is influenced by how much use they will get. If it's only occasional use, or if you're undecided on your future water feature requirement, the simplest option is to use some suitably coloured thick felt or fleece. Fleece is preferable because it has less tendency to crease.

Another material that is commonly used as a basis for water features (and also roads) is butyl rubber. It's available in various grades and is intended for use as pond linings or damp course membranes. However, for this particular project I decided to try a different material: vinyl floor tiles.

CONSTRUCTION

It's relatively simple to create straight lengths of river or canal: just mark it out and cut a straight line. However, meandering rivers or river bends are a little more involved. For my rivers I use a pair of callipers set to the appropriate width, and trace the shape of my river section onto the tile (Figure 104).

Obviously, if you have already made or bought some bridges, make sure that you don't make your river sections too wide; but ideally follow nature by making your rivers first and then your bridges.

Use a blue, dark green or brown tile depending on the type of water represented, and if the flow is to be fast moving you can simulate this by lightly painting or airbrushing thin streaks of white following the shape of the river.

You may also decide to suggest a river bank (Figure 105). My technique is to just run a line of PVA glue along the edges of the vinyl tile and sprinkle on static grass or flock which prevents a sudden change from land to water and, if the static grass or flock matches the surrounding terrain, will help to blend the river in too. One advantage of representing the banks with just a line of glue and some static grass is that it keeps the height relatively shallow, so you can turn the tile over, brush on PVA glue, sprinkle on fine sand, paint it and you have a scenery piece that is a river section on one side and a road on the other. Making a pond follows the same basic procedure (Figure 106).

Figure 104:
Marking out the river section using callipers.

Figure 105:
A river section with bank.

Figure 106:
A pond complete with ducking stool … but no victim as yet.

Figure 107:
Olustee.
(Battlegroup South)

The guys from Battlegroup South adopted a different technique for representing water. For their *Olustee* American Civil War game (Figure 107), they cut sheets of acrylic, painted one side dark brown, and once it was completely dried, turned it over and added static grass to create banks and islands.

If you want to represent a marshy area, choose a dark brown or green tile and add patches of static grass or lichen to represent weeds and other vegetation. For added effect you can incorporate random items that failed to sink completely below the surface, such as branches or even a body!

Whether you use a length of blue felt, a floor tile or a ready-made terrain and river tile, you can further enhance the overall effect by gluing some bristles from a garden broom to a piece of clear acetate (such as is used for packaging figures), to represent clumps of reeds (Figure 108).

Figure 108: Broom bristles glued to clear acetate to represent reeds.

8

ISLANDS, CLIFFS AND HILLS

E ssentially these three items of scenery are very similar, so you need to make the same basic design decisions:

- Will they be purely aesthetic, or will they form an important part of the scenario? For example, will they be accessible to troops? If so there needs to be a method of reaching the top, either in the form of a path or roadway, or at least one face of the hill or cliff needs to have a gentle slope up which troops and possibly vehicles can move.
- Will they form part of defences? If so, you'll have to ensure that there's enough flat surface to position walls or a tower or whatever. I'd avoid making hills with permanent defences integrated into them unless you feel that you'll be using that particular set up regularly.

PROJECT 4: An Island

This project is primarily about demonstrating basic cliff-making techniques. As already stated, so far as the edges are concerned, island cliffs and rugged hills are very similar, so the techniques in this project are equally applicable

Figure 109:
A *Dystopian Wars* Prussian naval and airship base.

to both. I have concentrated on the cove area of an island because it includes more detail than the cliffs alone (Figure 109).

MATERIALS
- High density foam
- Fine sand
- Static grass

CONSTRUCTION
The technique you use for initially cutting out your island depends primarily on its height. If the material used is not too thick, the least messy option is to use a hot wire cutter. Otherwise you'll have to roughly cut the shape using a compass saw and finish it off with the hot wire cutter. I've said it before, but cutting high density foam using a saw is messy, so if you want to maintain domestic harmony, you should do the cutting outside. And if you use a hot wire cutter, work in a well-ventilated area or outside. Wearing a mask is also recommended to avoid inhaling any of the vapour created when cutting the foam.

With the main island piece cut out, the next step was to carefully cut a pathway into the side of the cliff to allow access to the top of the island (Figure 110). As always when cutting a gradient, take time out to place a figure on it to ensure that it doesn't slide down.

Figure 110:
The access path.

Using the hot wire cutter, shape and add more detail to the surface of your cliffs. You'll notice a few over-enthusiastic cuts into the cliff face, but it's not a problem because they can easily be filled. However don't do any filling until you've finished all hot wire cutting in that area because hot wire cutters don't cut cleanly through filler.

The next step is texturing the top of the island and this depends on the purpose to which you intend to put your island, as well as the scale of the figures or vehicles. My island was to feature an airbase, so the top surface had to be flat; but if you want a more rugged appearance, make some suitably sized craggy sided hills, and glue them in place. If you push cocktail sticks through the hill and into the island this will help to keep the hills in position while the glue dries. In fact when gluing together layers of foam or similar material, I leave the cocktail sticks in place as I find it creates a much stronger joint than glue alone.

As for scale, I intended using the island with the *Dystopian Wars* range of ships and aircraft (which are relatively small scale), so I decided that any texturing of the surface would look over-scale. Another consideration is that if you intend to place buildings on the upper surface of the island, coarse texturing won't allow the buildings to sit flat which always looks odd in my opinion. For larger scale models you could add interest to the top surface of your island by giving it a coat of PVA glue followed by a light sprinkling of fine sand.

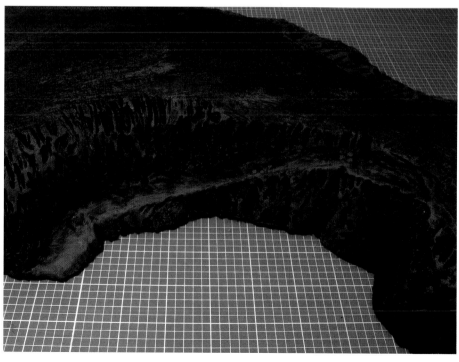

Figure 111:
The island after a black basecoat and grey drybrush.

Figure 112:
The finished island.

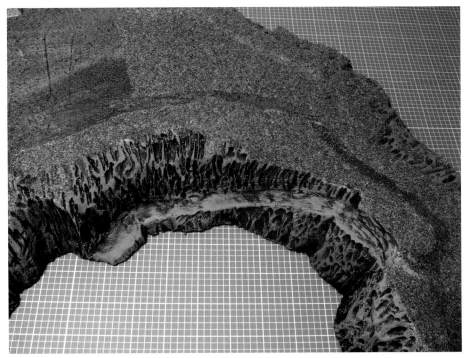

Figure 113:
Midway: an
alternative view.
(Jonathan Rogers)

Once I was satisfied with the overall look of the island, I gave it a coat of matt black, followed by a grey drybrush (Figure 111). Finally, decide which areas of the island will be grassed and give these areas a coat of PVA glue followed by a sprinkling of static grass. Adding the grass can be a convenient way of delineating roads or tracks (Figure 112).

Another approach to creating islands is to build not just the island itself, but to incorporate the surrounding coastal water so that you can integrate the breakers and white water as was the case with an alternative *Midway* game by Jonathan Rogers (Figure 113).

Hills

As already covered, the creation of rugged edged hills use the same technique as for the cliffs of an island. However if you want your hills to feature a gentler slope, just cut shallower angles and don't engrave cliff detail (Figure 114). This hill was created to accomodate a Saxon Great Hall, and was sized to fit in the corner of a customer's pre-existing terrain setup.

Figure 114:
A small hill.

Whenever you're building terrain and scenery, never throw away high density foam offcuts (Figure 115). Even small pieces can be useful as isolated rocky outcrops or – if nothing else – to test different adhesives or paints.

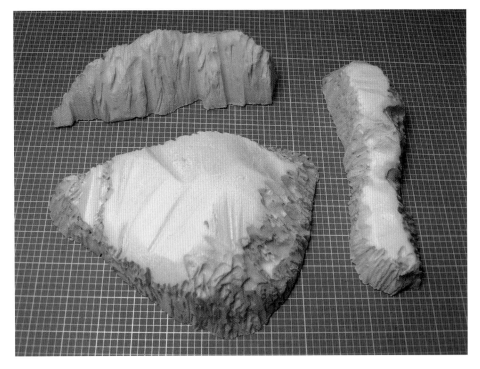

Figure 115:
Even offcuts of high density foam can be useful.

9

TREES

Y ou can purchase some truly excellent model trees, either ready-made or in kit form, but like buildings, if you want more than a handful they can work out extremely expensive. Basic trees are easy to make, so why not save your money and spend it items you cannot make yourself, such as figures?

Chancellorsville by the Newbury & Reading Wargames Society included a large number of trees, and at around £2 each for a commercially available tree, must have represented a significant investment (Figure 116).

In my opinion most trees seen on wargame tables are too small. Next time you get the opportunity, take a look at some trees, and compare their height with a standing figure. For example, if the average height for a mature oak tree is 30 to 40 metres, and assuming that a based 28mm figure is the equivalent of 2 metres tall, then the model tree should be about 30cm tall!

Small trees are fine if you're trying to create an orchard or a newly planted plantation, but if your battle is taking place in an area of mature woodland, then you need big trees.

Figure 116:
Jackson springs the trap at *Chancellorsville.* (*The Newbury and Reading Wargames Society*)

Before starting to make trees, you should think about their basing. Do you want individual trees or groups? I prefer single trees because that gives me more flexibility, but there is a case for both. Single trees tend to need proportionately larger bases to prevent them falling over, and it can be more difficult to clearly delineate the edges of wooded areas, which is why many wargamers lay out a sheet of green felt or cloth onto which the trees are placed.

As well as creating woodland or forests, trees can be a feature or a mini-diorama in their own right, as was the case with *Ayacucho 1824* by the South London Warlords, which very effectively flew the flag for 20mm soft plastic figures (Figure 117).

Most wargame rules include restrictions covering visibility into and out of woodland, so if you incorporate a line of lichen, or small stones at the appropriate distance in from the edge of the woodland this area can be easily defined without the need for measuring ... and cuts down on debate.

Before getting down to making a tree, always ensure that you've got an appropriately sized container in which to store it. Although my way of making trees results in some relatively durable scenery, it's still important to store it well.

Figure 117:
*Ayacucho 1824.
(The South London
Warlords)*

PROJECT 5: A Simple Tree

MATERIALS
- Small twigs and branches
- Rubberised horsehair
- Different coloured green flock or sponge
- Thick card (you can also use cork or vinyl tiles, thin plywood or mdf).

CONSTRUCTION
Select suitable twigs or branches and cut them to the length required (Figure 118). If you can't find a suitable shape, select one twig to form the core of your tree and glue smaller twigs onto it using a hot melt glue gun until you're satisfied with the overall appearance of the tree (Figure 119). To help hold the additional twigs in place, you can wrap thin wire around the joint and apply hot wax over the joint (Figure 120).

Cut out a base from thin mdf, plywood or even thick card. Remember that any porous material will have a tendency to bend if you only glue or paint on one side. Large or tall trees can become unstable so I try to make my bases to the same overall size as the maximum spread of the branches. For this particular project, I used offcuts of vinyl floor tile. Finding an effective glue to fix different materials together can be difficult. Wood to vinyl tiles is definitely one of those combinations, but I used my hot melt glue gun, which worked perfectly.

Figure 118:
Twigs will become trees!

Figure 119:
A close-up of tree assembly.

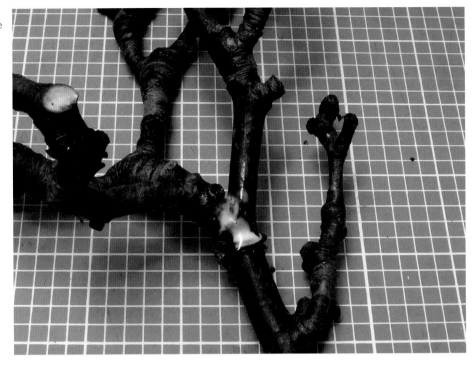

Figure 120:
Hot wax works well when gluing together different materials.

Take some rubberised horsehair and pull it apart. Carefully paint the branches of the tree with thinned PVA glue and slide the horsehair onto the branches. You may have to repeat this process until you're happy with the overall shape of the tree. This is an extremely messy procedure, not least because the PVA will drip off the branches and onto the base. To avoid the glue going to waste, I added more PVA to the base in the places where the excess from adding the foliage hadn't dripped, and sprinkled on some fine sand (Figure 121).

Spray the tree with matt black. You can brush on the paint, but you're likely to dislodge the horsehair, so spraying is the best option. A look around you or on the Internet will show that the wood of trees may be many colours … but never pure brown! Once the black undercoat has thoroughly dried, drybrush the trunks of the tree with grey to pick out the texture of the wood. I also add patches of dark green to represent moss or lichen. In the northern hemisphere, moss grows primarily on the north side of the trunk where there is less sunlight; in the southern hemisphere the location is reversed.

The next step is to add the foliage. For most of my trees I use Woodland Scenics' clump foliage. It's basically finely chopped and suitably coloured small pieces of sponge. I'm told that if it's not fine enough you can put it into a food blender for a few seconds. It might work – I've not tried it – but if you want to give it a go, I suggest that you wait until you're alone in the house, as commandeering kitchen equipment for hobby purposes never goes down well!

Figure 121:
A tree with horsehair added and fine sand sprinkled onto the base.

There is a wide range of clump foliage available so you can represent a tree in spring or summer. An interesting alternative is dried moss, which you can buy in blocks from garden centres (Figure 122). The easiest way to prepare the moss for use is to break it up by rubbing it between your hands over a piece of newspaper. Dried moss is also very good for representing ground cover.

There are several different ways of gluing foliage. My preferred method of gluing foliage in place is to make a 50/50 mix of PVA glue and water, spray this over the basic tree and then sprinkle on the clump foliage. To finish off, I lightly spray the foliage with hair lacquer and sprinkle on static grass. Whatever foliage you use, it's a good idea to apply it over a sheet of newspaper to make it easier to collect any excess for re-use.

To complete the tree, the base is painted to match the terrain, and patches of static grass, dried moss and clump foliage are glued in place (Figure 123).

And that is pretty much it: a cheap and easy to make tree. All you've got to do now is complete the remaining hundred or so to create your forest.

As with most scenery making projects, there are nearly always different techniques, and tree making is no exception. One alternative approach is that used by Mick Allan and Bradley Taylor for their game, *The Siege of Exeter 1939* (Figure 124). They used proprietary tree trunks but instead of using rubberised horsehair followed by sprinkling on fine clump foliage, they just used large clumps and glued them directly to the trunk and branches.

Figure 122:
Dried moss.

Figure 123:
A tree complete
with foliage.

Figure 124:
Trees in *The Siege
of Exeter 1939.*
(*Mick Allan and
Bradley Taylor*)

10

Unsurprisingly, the appearance of walls is dictated by their primary construction material and the cheapest material was nearly always that found locally. So walls are more regionalised than you might imagine; this chapter shows you how to construct three of the most common styles.

There are a number of practical design considerations to resolve which apply to whatever type of wall you intend to build:

- Can it be shot over?
- Can it be clambered over or will ladders be needed to scale it?
- Will it be intact or battle-damaged?

Regarding the latter question, I find it a good idea to make intact and damaged wall sections that you can easily interchange as the battle progresses. And it's much better to make all the wall sections in the same session to ensure that they match in terms of the wall's surface, the base texturing and overall colour.

Needless to say, the various techniques presented in this chapter for making walls, can apply equally well when you're making buildings. As you gain more experience, you'll no doubt discover new and different techniques, so never be afraid to experiment, and if you find what you believe to be a really useful technique, don't keep it to yourself!

PROJECT 6: A Dry Stone Wall

Dry stone walling is a technique so named because no mortar or other 'gluing' substance is used, and it has been practised for hundreds of years (Figure 125). It is commonly seen in upland areas or other places where suitable stones can be found. Examples of dry stone walling can be seen in locations as far apart as the city walls at Cusco in south east Peru, to the Lion Gate at Mycenae.

MATERIALS:
- High density foam
- Thick card or mounting board
- Pins

The thickness of your foam depends on the scale of figures with which you intend to use the wall, but I find that 0.3 or 0.5cm is a good starting point and you can always laminate pieces together if needed.

CONSTRUCTION

To determine the height of your wall, first decide if it needs to be shot over, or if it will form a barrier over which troops must climb.

Cut a length of high density foam to the length and height of your wall section, and a piece of thick card to the same length for the base. Rest the wall on the base and if required, double check that a based figure can see or shoot over it (Figure 126).

Using suitable reference material as a guide, use an old ballpoint pen or something similar to engrave the pattern into the wall (Figure 127). Dry stone walls usually comprise two lines of stones, with larger stones placed at right angles to tie the two lines of stones together. These two lines are then held together by capping stones placed at right angles across the top. Engrave these across the top of your wall (Figure 128).

Glue the wall to its base. For added strength, I draw the centreline of the wall on the card base, drill a series of small holes along the line and then, after gluing the wall section in place, push a series of pins into the wall from underneath. Next give the base a coat of filler and once dry, brush on PVA and sprinkle on sand and fine gravel to give it texture (Figure 129). When adding the texture, remember the scale of the figures that will most often be used with the walls. What might be an inconsequential pebble to a 28mm heroic giant will be an impassable boulder to a 10mm figure.

101

Figure 126:
Checking whether an archer would be able to shoot over the wall before starting to engrave the stonework.

Figure 127:
Using a ballpoint pen to engrave the stonework.

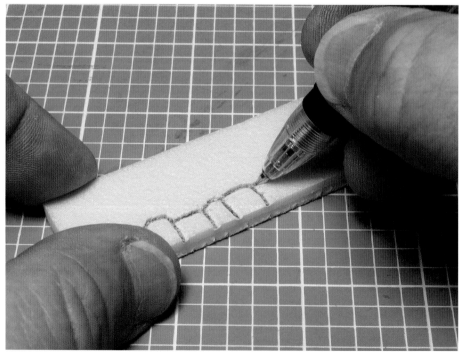

Figure 128:
Finishing off the stonework on one side.

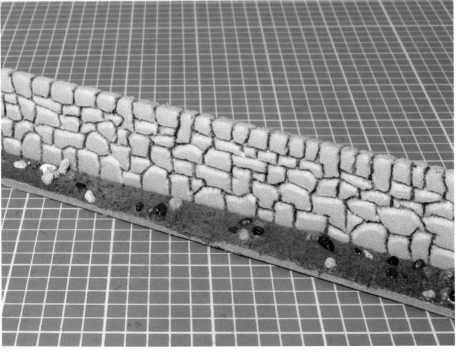

Figure 129:
A wall with a textured base.

Paint the base and the wall with a black undercoat, making sure to get the paint right into the engraved lines of the wall. Don't use aerosol spray paint because it attacks the foam.

Drybrush the base with dark brown followed by a very light drybrush of pale cream. If in doubt as to the colours to use for the base, paint it to match your terrain.

My wall was drybrushed with successively lighter coats of grey, and random stones were picked out in contrasting greys (Figure 130). Don't overdo this technique otherwise you'll finish up with a wall that looks like a cross between crazy paving and a patchwork quilt.

Depending on the age of the wall, you can brush slightly watered down PVA glue into some of the gaps in the stonework and sprinkle on green flock or static grass to represent moss. Remember that in exposed areas, the moss tends to grow on the side of the wall away from the sun in shady locations so that it doesn't dry out.

Thinking about the small details of scenery making, it's a good idea to create your own database of useful images. Not just general views of buildings, but close-ups of particular details too (Figure 131).

A different approach, instead of engraving the stonework into the surface, is to glue small pebbles onto the wall. Pin and glue the wall to a card base following the technique described previously. Stone walls tend to have larger stones at the bottom so I first run a line of hot wax along the lower section

Figure 130:
A finished wall.

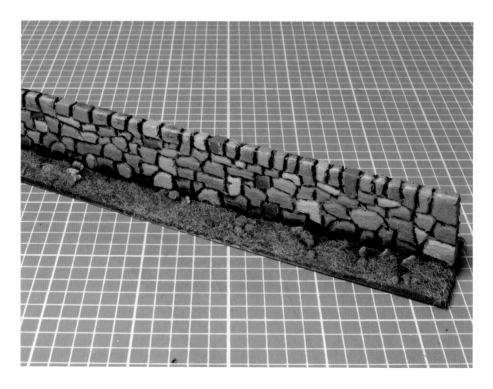

Figure 131:
Stone walls don't just come in grey!

Figure 132:
A different type of wall.

of the wall into which I press the stones. The wax sets very quickly and is a more efficient method of fixing the heavier stones at the base of the wall. The smaller stones are held in place using undiluted PVA glue. Texturing and painting the wall and base also follow the same procedure as before (Figure 132).

PROJECT 7: A Brick Wall

Unlike stone walls that usually feature irregularly shaped stones, brick walls are laid in regular patterns or bonds. There are many different bonds, some of which are better suited for particular applications. Before looking at several of the more widely used bonds, it's probably useful to be aware of some terminology relating to the bricks themselves, namely that the longest side of a brick is known as the 'stretcher', and the shortest side is the 'header'.

Figure 133:
Types of bond: A English, B Flemish, C Stretcher.

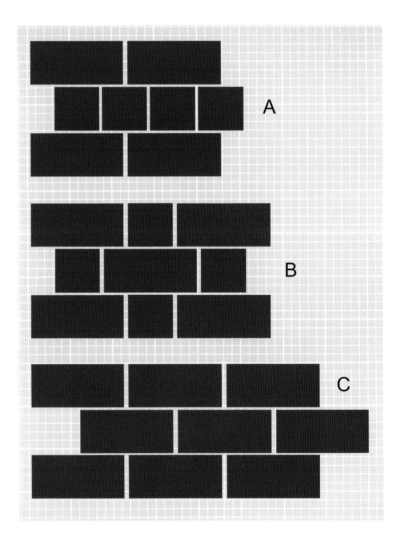

There are three common bonds or patterns of brickwork (Figure 133):

- English bond walls have alternate rows where in one row the bricks are laid with the header facing outwards, but in the next, the stretcher faces outwards. English bond makes for a particularly strong wall.
- Flemish bond walls have the bricks in each row alternating between stretcher and header, which results in a very strong double thickness wall.
- Stretcher bond walls are usually thin and generally need extra supports in the form of pillars or buttresses.

Having decided upon which bond your wall will have, the procedure is similar to that for creating dry stone walls: the brickwork is engraved into the foam.

MATERIALS
- High density foam
- Thick card or mounting board

As with stone walls, the thickness of your foam depends on the scale of figures with which you intend to use the wall, but I find that 0.3 to 0.5cm fits in with most scales.

CONSTRUCTION
Cut out your wall sections, and then cut suitable bases from mounting board. Since brickwork follows a more regular pattern than random stone, it will make the engraving easier if you lightly mark out the horizontal lines of your brickwork onto the wall, and then engrave the horizontal lines followed by the vertical ones.

Draw the centreline on the base, and drill a series of holes along it. Apply a line of No More Nails or other instant grab adhesive along the centre line. Position the wall in the adhesive. Blend the adhesive between the base and the wall, and push pins through the base at an angle to hold the wall in place.

Once the adhesive has fully dried, brush over the base with diluted PVA glue and sprinkle on fine sand and perhaps add a few large pebbles. The bases for the walls need to match your terrain. I always start with an overall undercoat of black followed by drybrushing; usually a dark brown first followed by a lighter colour to pick out detail (Figure 134). If in doubt, consult your records for the colours you have used for your terrain and get as close to that specification as possible.

The colour of bricks can vary a lot depending on the area, so carry out a bit of research to determine the most suitable colours. It adds interest to pick out a few bricks in a slightly contrasting colour. Next add static grass to the base and set aside the wall to dry thoroughly. The final stage is to add the mortar. My method is to use powdered chalk and brush it over the brickwork

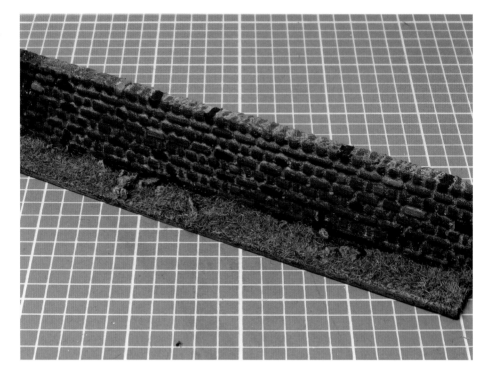

and into the cracks. Carefully wipe over the surface of the bricks so that the powdered chalk remains only in the gaps between the bricks. I'm told that you can also use talcum powder, although I've not tried it myself. At least it would make the walls smell quite fragrant. And to seal the powdered chalk in place, I lightly spray matt varnish over the walls.

PROJECT 8: An Adobe Wall

Another type of brick used in the construction of walls is adobe, which is a mixture of sand, clay, water and straw blocked and dried in the sun. Walls built using adobe were often given a thin coat of plaster made from mud or stucco for protection, making them relatively simple to create.

Bear in mind that unreinforced adobe walls have relatively limited loadbearing capability, which is why you rarely see adobe walls or buildings higher than two storeys.

MATERIALS
• High density foam or foamboard
• Thick card
• Filler
• Fine sand

CONSTRUCTION

If you want to create a wall with exposed brickwork, either because of age or battle damage, use foam because you can engrave into its surface. Cut your length of wall from high density foam and also cut out any doors or windows. Engrave the brickwork where required (Figure 135), and apply a thin layer of filler to the rest of the wall. Alternatively you can PVA the walls leaving a space for exposed brickwork and sprinkle on fine sand (Figure 136).

The reason that I texture the wall before fitting it to a base is because this makes it easier to get a good coating of filler to the very bottom of the wall.

Once you've textured the sides and top of the wall, the next step is to base the wall on a piece of thick card. I nearly always use an instant grab adhesive, and for additional strength I drill a series of holes along the centreline of the base through which I insert pins to hold the wall section in place. Always smooth the adhesive at the base of the walls so that it blends in to the base.

Give the base a coating of PVA glue followed by a sprinkling of sand and a few boulders. Adobe walls are generally found in hot, arid areas where everything gets bleached by the sun, so for painting I start with a mid sand coloured undercoat, which is then drybrushed with successively lighter sand colours, finishing up with a very light drybrush of white. I also add a few patches of static grass to break up the walls a bit (Figure 137).

Figure 135: Engraved brickwork exposed through plaster.

Figure 136:
Exposed brickwork with plaster suggested by fine sand.

Figure 137:
Finished adobe wall sections.

11

FENCES AND SCREENS

The construction or design of fences is relatively similar the whole world over: a series of uprights are hammered into the ground, to which are attached horizontal bars. The timber used may be rough natural timber or machined planks. From a scenery making aspect, the design and construction of fences is very similar.

PROJECT 9: A Cross Rail Fence

MATERIALS
- Wood
- Thick card
- Pea shingle or small pebbles

The wood you use depends on the type of fence you're trying to create and the scale of model you'll use it with, but you'll need balsa, cocktail sticks, toothpicks or barbeque skewers.

CONSTRUCTION

If the ground is particularly hard or stony, it's often impossible to dig conventional post holes into the ground, so other construction methods have to be used. This project demonstrates one option.

The height of your fences depends on whether or not you intend troops to be able to shoot over it, in which case you take your height measurements from a suitably posed and based figure. The fence height is also influenced by whether they are intended to enclose crops or livestock.

As for the fence section width, I usually match mine to a base or movement tray frontage. It's always best to work on several fence sections at a time, and I tend to make enough fence sections to completely enclose an area. Draw the centre line and run a line of hot wax along it and then quickly press pebbles into the hot wax before it cools (Figure 138). If necessary, repeat this process. I used aquarium gravel in some appalling colours; if you do the same, don't worry, once it's painted it looks fine. It was cheap, and the fish didn't need it as much as me.

Give the bases a coating of PVA glue and sprinkle on fine sand. Once dry, coat the base with black and then give the stones a drybrush of mid grey (Figure 139). Don't worry if you drybrush the base, you'll be painting over it anyway.

Paint the base dark brown and then drybrush it with a pale cream, and then paint some areas of the base with PVA glue and apply static grass (Figures 140–141).

Figure 138:
Stoned fence
bases.

Figure 139:
Black undercoated
and grey
drybrushed bases.

Figure 140:
Painted bases.

Figure 141:
Bases with static grass added.

Figure 142:
Bases with
supports and rails.

Figure 143:
A fence with
supports in place.

Cut short lengths of balsa to make the crosspiece supports, and also longer pieces for the horizontal rails. Paint the supports and rails black and glue the supports astride the stones (Figures 142–143). Finally, glue the painted rails in place, and lightly drybrush the upper surfaces of the woodwork with pale grey (Figure 144).

PROJECT 10: A Split Rail or Snake Rail Fencing

Having said that fences are similar the whole world over, there's one fence type without which no self-respecting North American battlefield would be complete: the split rail or snake rail fence. Usually made from wooden logs split lengthwise to make rails, these rails were stacked on top of one another in a self-supporting zig-zag interlocking pattern (Figure 145).

This style of fence was particularly suited for use on hard or stony ground where it was difficult to dig holes for upright posts. It used a lot of wood compared to other types of fencing, so was only used in areas where there was plenty of suitable timber close to the location.

Figure 145:
Completed snake rail fences.

MATERIALS

- Wood – balsa, cocktail sticks, tooth picks or barbeque skewers
- Thick card
- Fine sand
- Static grass

CONSTRUCTION

As is often the case with wargaming, you need to make a slight compromise when designing and building your split rail fencing, because you'll have to include supporting uprights (otherwise it is extremely difficult to create and keep the necessary spacing between the horizontal rails).

Determine the ideal base size for your fence and cut out the bases from thick card or thin mdf. Cut a length of rail (I used toothpicks in the illustrated example) that will go slightly beyond the halfway point and rest it on a short temporary supporting piece (Figure 146). Cut another toothpick to the same length and glue it to the first toothpick and the card (Figure 147). Cut another supporting piece and rest another rail on it, only gluing the end that rests on the second rail (Figure 148). Then add a spacing piece on top of the second toothpick and lay on another rail (Figure 149).

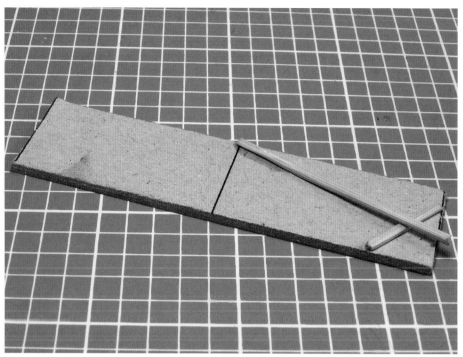

Figure 146:
Creating the first rail.

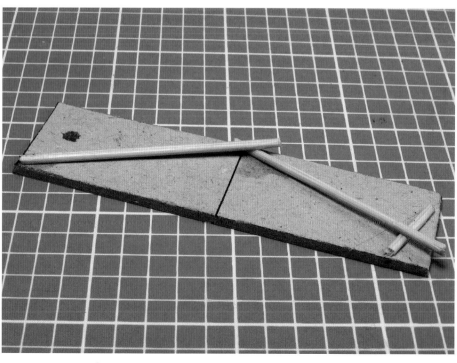

Figure 147:
Adding the next rail.

Figure 148:
The first rail,
second row.

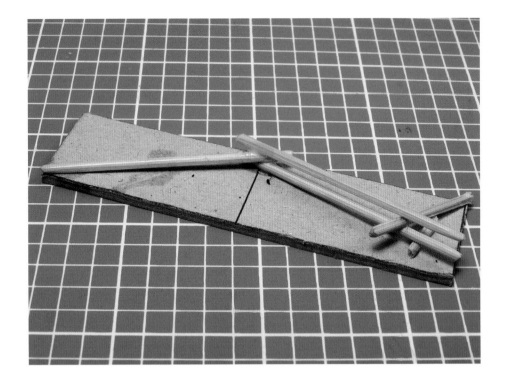

Figure 149:
Adding another
rail.

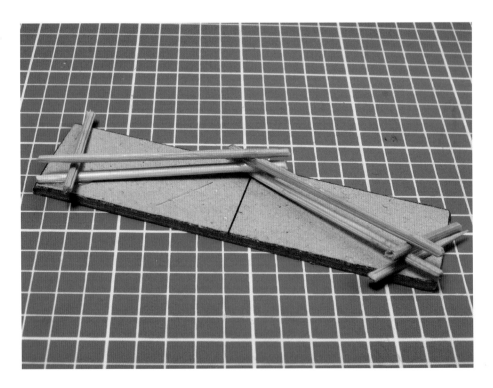

Repeat these steps until the fence is the required height. I only made my fences two rails high because I was intending to use them with 10mm figures. If you want to have more rails in the same height then you've got to use much thinner (and more fragile) components, but if you are going to use them with larger figures, continue the previous steps until the fence sections look correct compared to your based figures.

Once you're satisfied that your split rail fence is the right height, cut some short pieces of wood to make the vertical supporting uprights and glue them in position (Figure 150). Once the glue has dried, remove the temporary short supports.

The base was given a coating of PVA glue and sprinkled with sand. The fence and base were given a black undercoat, the rails were drybrushed grey and the ground was painted dark brown (Figure 151). For painting my base, I used Dulux Exotic Spice 2 as the base coat, and for my woodwork I used Dulux Flint.

Next, the base was lightly drybrushed with pale cream, and static grass added (Figure 152). With split rail fences, there's no need to make special corner pieces, you can just butt adjacent sections up together.

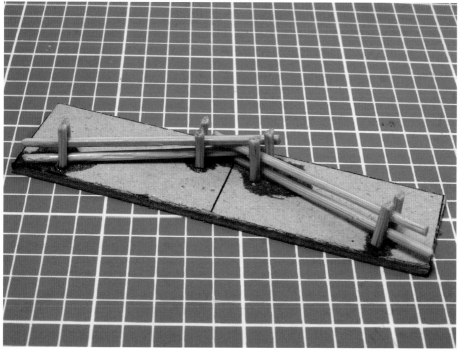

Figure 150:
The upright
supports added.

Figure 151:
Painting the fence
and base.

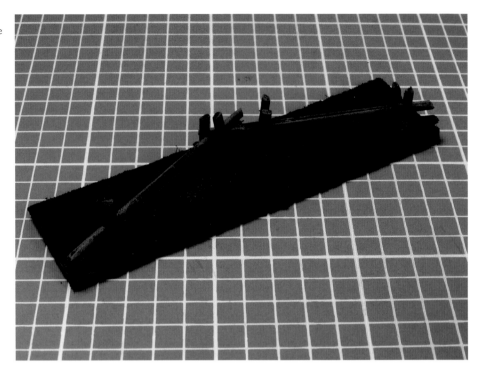

Figure 152:
Finished fence
sections.

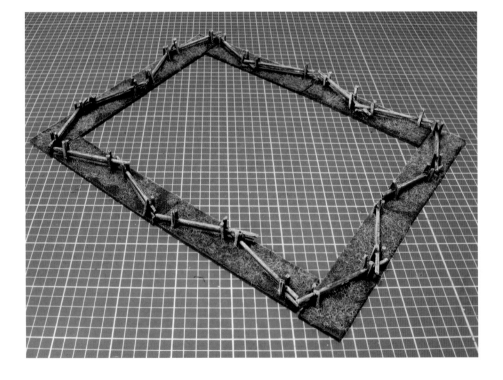

PROJECT 11: Brush Fences

MATERIALS
- Mounting board
- Toothpicks or barbeque skewers depending on the scale of the brush fences
- Brushwood screening
- Fine sand and pebbles

CONSTRUCTION
Brush fences sections are extremely simple to make (Figure 153). You start by making the base out of mounting board, and texture it with fine sand and pebbles as described previously. The base is painted to match your terrain and static grass is added.

Drill a series of holes, in pairs, astride the centreline of the base. Cut lengths of toothpick to the appropriate height, paint them black, drybrush them grey and glue them into the holes. Once the glue has set, cut lengths of brushwood screening and glue them between the uprights, and that's it!

Figure 153: Brushwood fencing.

PROJECT 12: Wattle Panels

Another form of fencing was the wattle screen or panel, made by weaving thin branches, either whole or in split lengths, between vertical wooden stakes (Figure 154).

MATERIALS
- Cocktail sticks, toothpicks, or barbeque skewers, depending on scale
- Thin textured paper
- Mounting board or thin mdf
- Fine sand and grit
- Static grass

CONSTRUCTION

The weave effect of the basic panels is created by sliding sticks alternately through slots cut into pieces of textured paper (Figure 155).

To make the wattle panel a series of horizontal cuts must be made, but they should not go right to the ends of each panel section (Figure 156). As with fencing, it's a good idea to make a series of panels in a single session.

Carefully cut along the horizontal lines. Cut out the individual panels and then thread the first upright through the slots (Figure 157). Thread the remaining uprights alternately through the slots (Figure 158). Trim the top

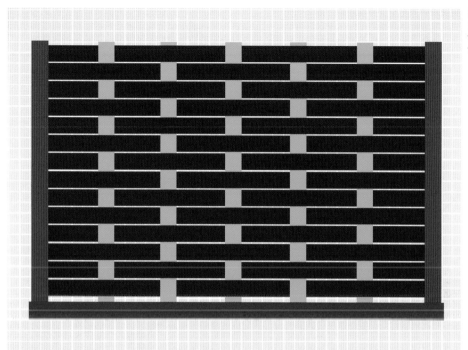

Figure 155:
Diagram showing the weave of wattle strips.

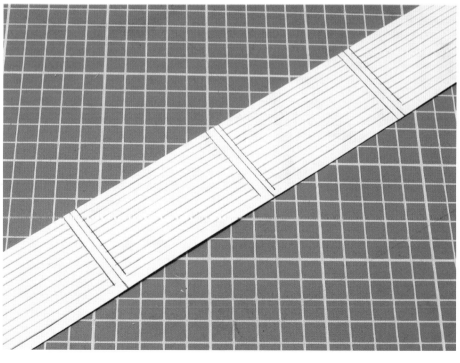

Figure 156:
A row of wattle panels ready for cutting.

Figure 157:
A basic panel with the first upright threaded in position.

Figure 158:
A basic panel with all the uprights threaded through.

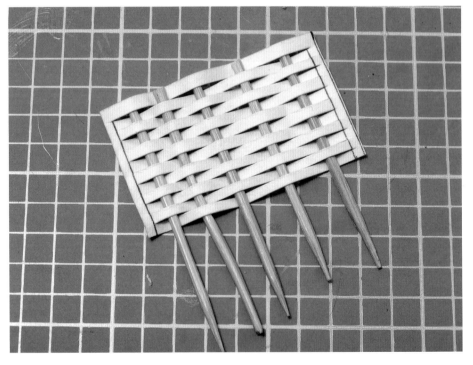

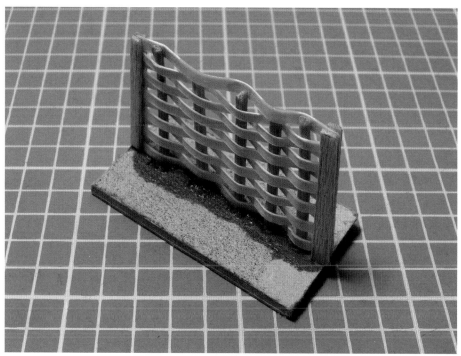

Figure 159:
A based wattle panel.

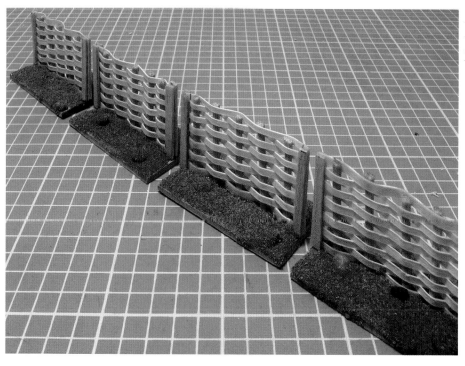

Figure 160:
Wattle panels as far as the eye can see … well, four of them.

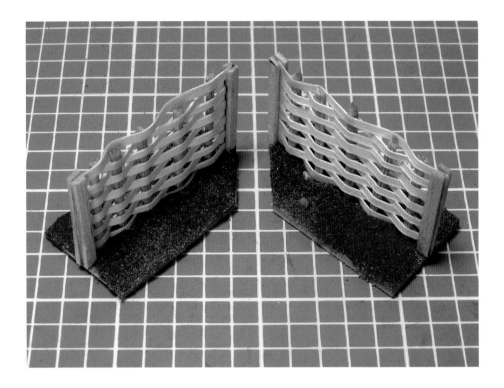

Figure 161:
Wattle panel
corner pieces.

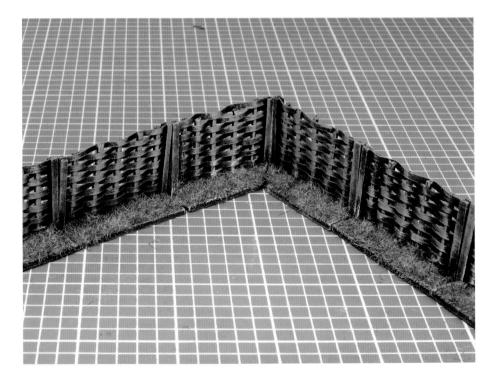

Figure 162:
Finished wattle
panels.

of the uprights as necessary. Cut a base and drill a series of holes along the centreline to match the poles, and glue the panel into position using PVA glue. Once the panel is securely glued in position, trim off any excess of the sticks so the base sits flat (Figure 159).

I added thin strips of balsa at each end of the panel to finish off the edges, but it's not strictly necessary (Figure 160). To make corner pieces, simply cut one end of your base at 45° and follow the technique already shown (Figure 161). My panels have their bases textured with fine sand with a few small pebbles added for good measure.

Undercoat the panels and base with black. You can use an aerosol spray but this can work out expensive because it's difficult to get the spray into the cracks (so you'll probably have to touch the panels up anyway).

My standard way to represent aged wood is to drybrush it mid grey followed by selectively lighter coats. For the ground I use the same colours as for my terrain, which usually consists of a dark brown drybrush followed by a drybrush using a pale cream; finally I apply random patches of PVA glue and sprinkle on static grass (Figure 162).

12

HEDGES

I have separated hedges into two basic groups: cultivated hedges, and wild hedges. In the second group I also include the bocage of Normandy that proved such a challenge to the Allied invasion forces after the D-Day landings in Normandy, 1944.

PROJECT 13: A Cultivated Hedge

Relatively tidy, this type of hedge is probably less visually interesting on the wargames table than 'wild hedges', but they are very easy and quick to construct (Figure 163).

MATERIALS
- Green pan scouring pads
- Coloured flock
- Thick card
- Fine sand and grit
- Static grass

Figure 163: Napoleon's Old Grumblers in 10mm march past a hedgerow.

For hedges intended for use with small figures – 15mm or less – I use scouring pads, but for larger figures I tend to use synthetic wire wool.

CONSTRUCTION

First, decide on the height and length of your hedge. Then cut out your bases from mounting board and mark the centre line. Take a scouring pad and cut out your length of hedge; carefully run a line of hot glue along the centreline and press the hedge firmly into the glue. Be careful because the hot glue will – unsurprisingly – be hot!

Apply a coat of PVA glue to the base and sprinkle on fine sand with a few small pebbles or gravel. Paint the hedge and base matt black and set aside to dry thoroughly. Drybrush the hedge and the base in dark brown, followed by a pale cream drybrush of the base to enhance the texture. Brush PVA glue over the top and sides of the hedge and sprinkle on scatter material or flock (Figures 164–165).

An alternative technique for slightly larger scale hedges is to use synthetic wire wool pads as the basis for the hedge. Synthetic wire wool blocks are quite wide so you probably won't need a base, but the painting and the flocking process remain the same.

Figure 164:
A completed hedge.

PROJECT 14: Bocage

There's one particular hedge that we must not forget… bocage. There are several interpretations of the word, but basically 'bocage' refers to countryside made up of mixed woodland, pasture and fields, separated by narrow lanes enclosed by high berms or banks on top of which are hedgerows sometimes interspersed with trees (Figure 166). The banks upon which the hedges or trees sit are sometimes formed from compacted earth, sometimes from rocks and sometimes from a mixture of both.

MATERIALS
- Oasis® foam (this is the material used by florists in dried flower arranging)
- Sand
- Fine gravel or cat litter
- Static grass
- Rubberised horse hair
- Cocktail sticks or toothpicks
- Coloured flock

Rubberised horse hair may be purchased from modelmaking material suppliers, but if you want large quantities try an upholsterer as it is often used for filling cushions.

Figure 166:
1/72nd scale
Valiant British
infantry cautiously
make their way
through a section
of bocage.

CONSTRUCTION

Each section of your bocage must fit accurately with the adjacent one, so you need to create a template from thick card for the ends or cross-section of the banks; but before you can do that, you need to decide upon the dimensions of your bocage. It's clear from a quick browse of the Internet that there was no standardised bocage. The height of the bank could range from 1.8 to 3m, to which must be added the hedge and possible trees and shrubs, which could result in a total height of around 5m. To put this into some kind of perspective, a Tiger I tank was about 3m high. It was clear that bocage constituted a major obstacle to the movement of AFVs, and there are many contemporary photographs showing AFVs crossing open fields rather than being constricted in the narrow lanes edged with impenetrable high banks and hedges.

A further consideration before deciding on the dimensions of your template, is that since the Second World War is so popular with wargamers (to the extent that some wargamers have armies in more than one scale) by compromising slightly, you might be able to use your bocage for more than scale (Figure 167).

You have a wide choice of material from which to make the bank. Whichever material you use, cut it into convenient lengths. I use Oasis, which is the material used in dried flower arrangements. It's easy to cut and shape, but if you have some high density foam or similar material then you can use that instead.

131

Figure 167:
A template where (a) represents the approximate scale height of an AFV.

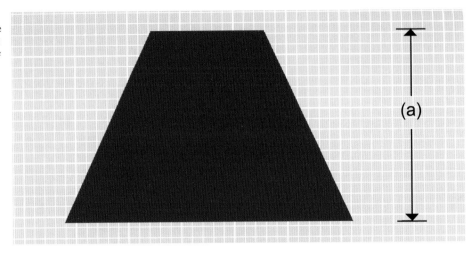

(a)

Cut your material into convenient lengths; if you use Oasis you're fairly limited as it's usually sold in blocks about 23cm x 11cm x 8cm. To cut the Oasis I used a snap-off blade knife and just extended the blade segments until it was long enough to cut right through. If you're using a denser material you may prefer to use a hot wire cutter.

I first cut my Oasis into blocks with a profile to match the untrimmed shape of my template (Figure 168), namely 5.5cm x 4cm and to the full

Figure 168:
Use the card template to create the correct gradient of the slopes.

length of the block, and then drew around the template at both ends of the section.

Carefully cut the Oasis to create the sloping banks. I used my snap-off blade knife again which easily cut through the material. Cutting the angled banks is a little tricky but it will be fine as long as you take your time and carefully follow your guidelines. The most important areas are those at each end where the adjacent sections join up. I started by accurately cutting the profiles at each end and then working towards the middle. The best technique is to carefully shave away material until you're satisfied with the final shape (Figure 169).

If you're making a corner section, start by creating the two adjacent pieces and gluing them together at a right angle, but only cut the outer slope of the bank (Figure 170). The reason for cutting the outer slopes is because I always use cocktail sticks or toothpicks as well as PVA glue to hold the pieces together and if you fix the two components together, it's likely that when you come to cut the slope you'll be trying to cut through the sticks!

Using the existing slopes and the template guidelines, finish off the slope on the outer and inner faces of the bank. Any gaps can easily be filled using ready-mixed filler. Once you have resolved the shape and profile of your banks you can consider how to treat their surfaces. Some references for bocage state that the core of the banks were piles of locally gathered stone (Figure 171). It's up to you whether or not to include exposed stones and

Figure 169:
The bocage banks cut.

rocks in the banks; if you do and you're using Oasis it's really easy to add stones: simply spread PVA glue along the lower front face of the bank and carefully push pieces of cat litter or gravel into the material. Be patient with this process – particularly if using cat litter – as it has a tendency to stick more to your fingers than to the Oasis, but it does work. Bear in mind that locally sourced stones are likely to be rough, so don't be tempted to use regular or round stones such as you'd find on a beach. Wait until the stones are securely glued in place and then carefully brush PVA glue over the sides and top edge of the bank. If you're making end pieces, PVA the end face too, but otherwise keep the end faces free of glue so that they butt up to the adjacent bank more accurately. Sprinkle sand over the bank and leave it to dry thoroughly (Figure 172).

In my experience, it's better to paint the banks before adding the hedges and other foliage. Give the bank a matt black undercoat using slightly thinned emulsion paint. When the undercoat has thoroughly dried, drybrush the bank with dark brown, followed by a light cream. Next pick out some of the exposed stones in mid grey and then drybrush them pale grey. Decide how much grass you want on your banks, which is largely dependent on how old the bank is: the older it is, the more overgrown you should make it.

Coat selected areas of the bank with PVA glue and then sprinkle on static grass until you're satisfied with the effect. Remember that the hedge and foliage on top of the bank will cover most of the top surface of the bank so

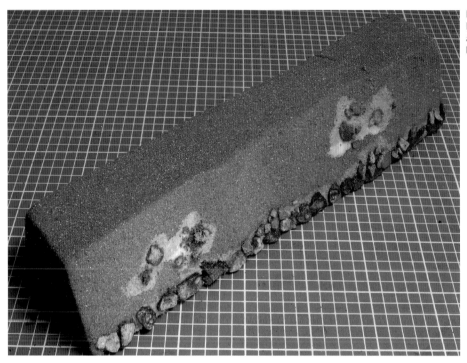

Figure 171:
Rough stones are
added to a bocage
bank.

Figure 172:
A sanded bank
section.

if you want to save on static grass, just put it along the exposed edges of the
top of the bank (Figure 173).

The material to use for the hedges on top of the bank will depend on the
size of the figures that you'll be using with it. Rubberised horsehair is a good
choice for 20mm figures or larger. But for smaller figures you might find that
synthetic wire wool gives a better scale result. This is supplied in a block that
can be carefully split and cut to make smaller sections.

Cut a piece of rubberised horsehair to the length of your bank section
and gently pull the horsehair apart to create a more irregular, unkempt
appearance. Place it on top of the bank. Position a figure or vehicle in front
of it, and then trim the horsehair so that the combined bank and hedge look
right. I push cocktail sticks painted black through the horsehair and into the
bank to hold the horsehair in place. Once you're satisfied with the look of the
hedge, spray it matt black followed by a light drybrush of brown to provide a
subtle contrast, and glue the hedge to the bank. To add foliage to the hedge,
brush on a coat of PVA glue and then sprinkle on green flock (Figure 174).

To add variety to your bocage sections, you can add small trees by following
the general instructions in Chapter Nine, applying glue to the lower section
of the completed tree trunk and pushing it through the hedge into the bank
itself (Figure 175). Be careful when increasing the overall height of your
bocage in case it starts to totally overwhelm your figures and vehicles.

Figure 174:
The completed
bocage piece.

Figure 175:
A bocage section
with tree.

13

GATES

To be honest, I don't often make gates. After all, from a wargamer's point of view, gates seldom need to open or close; troops arrive at the obstruction and cross it, they're not going to bother to look for a gate … and I doubt that the last soldier through will bother to close the gate behind them, so from the aspect of gameplay, gates are basically irrelevant (Figure 176). However, I feel that the inclusion of a simple gate adds to the aesthetics of the terrain. The type of gate used to allow access through a fence or wall depended on what was behind the wall, and what you were trying to keep out. Often a simple wooden bar or removable panel was all that was needed, but on other occasions a more solid gate was required. These gates were described by the number of horizontal bars on them: the most common types were three and five bar gates.

Figure 176:
Clearly this gate failed to separate livestock from crops!

PROJECT 15: A Three Bar Gate

MATERIALS
- Balsa
- Mounting board

CONSTRUCTION
Cut your base to size, and apply a texture by coating the base with PVA glue sprinkled with fine sand. Paint the base to match your terrain.

The gate is a simple balsa frame that fits between two upright posts. To allow for the diagonal bar and horizontals they must be half the thickness of the uprights (Figure 177). It is easiest to paint the gate before gluing it to the base. If you feel so inclined, you can even model an open gate to put in position if you want to add a bit more animation to your scenery.

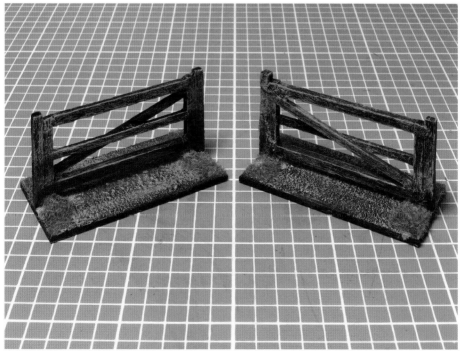

Figure 177: Showing both sides of a three bar gate.

14

CULTIVATED FIELDS

aving created your walls, fences and hedges, it might be a good idea to have something to be enclosed by them. As is always the case, the raw material you use depends upon the scale of your figures. Yellow fake fur is often used to represent cornfields when using 28mm figures or larger, as used in a Franco Prussian war game by the South Somerset Wargames Group (Figure 178).

An alternative material used is coir door matting. If you want to avoid giving yourself extra work, don't buy one with wording or other designs it. The South Dorset Military Society used a piece of doormat in their game *Cornwallis at Brandywine* (Figure 179).

Although this material tends to be used with larger scale figures due to its height, it can successfully be used with smaller scales, as was the case with Jon Soper and Steve Pearce's 15mm Marlburian game (Figure 180).

Yet another option is to use artificial grass (Figure 181) which can be purchased in a wide variety of finishes, making it suitable for almost any scale of figures: long grass, short grass, densely packed grass, even a 1:1 scale lawn!

Figure 178:
Prussian troops advance into a fake fur cornfield.
(*The South Somerset Wargames Group*)

Figure 179:
Cornwallis at Brandywine.
(The South Dorset Military Society)

Figure 180:
A section of coconut doormat standing in for a cornfield during a 15mm Marlburian game.
(Jon Soper and Steve Pearce)

Figure 181:
A field made from
artificial grass.

Figure 182:
The field has been
tilled, but there's
no sign of the
crops as yet.

Figure 183:
A ribbed doormat field of growing crops enclosed by suitable fencing.

Figure 184:
A field awaiting ploughing.

When creating fields with tall crops growing in them, it is aesthetically more pleasing if you cut the field into pieces, similar in width to that of an appropriate number of single bases or a movement tray, so that you can remove sections of the crops as your troops march through. For planted but not fully grown fields of crops, or for use with smaller scale figures, ribbed doormats can give an interesting effect (Figures 182–183). Just cut the doormat to size, enclose it with suitable fencing and that's it. And with crops growing, we need to enclose the field to keep them safe: the construction of fences is covered in Chapter Eleven.

An interesting additional use for these ribbed doormats can be found if you turn them over. The underside lacks the ridges, but has enough texture to drybrush and simulate the effect of an unploughed field (Figure 184).

15

ROADS

oads are one of the most common pieces of scenery on a wargames table, and you must decide whether to integrate them into your terrain or have them as separate components. The latter option offers far more choice, but this is balanced by aesthetics: to me, roads look more realistic if they are a part of the terrain, but for maximum flexibility in use, I usually make all my scenery separate from my terrain.

However, for those wargamers who prefer to have their roads built-in, let's look at a couple of different approaches depending on your base terrain.

Integrating Roads into a Terrain Cloth

If you're using fleece or felt for your basic terrain, the easiest way to include roads is by painting them onto the surface, but I've never been overly impressed with that approach.

For me, the ideal material for a terrain cloth is a throw, because it has a pile. Creating a road can be fairly easily achieved by using a pair of electric hair trimmers to shave off the fur (Figure 185). With the roads cut into

Figure 185:
15mm AWI British cavalry making their way along a road shaved into a throw.

Figure 186:
A road integrated
into a fur throw
using flexible
acrylic sealant.
(*The South East
Essex Military
Society*)

the cloth, you can then paint them to further distinguish them from the surrounding ground.

A technique used by SEEMS was to give their shaved roads a coating of flexible acrylic sealer into which they added a suitable texture – in this case ruts from the passage of wheeled wagons – but they could have easily been tyre or tank tracks as appropriate (Figure 186).

Both these examples relate to unmade roads. Tarmac roads are not so easily integrated into cloth terrain because their surfaces are generally noticeably smoother than those of unmade roads, and even the texture of the bare throw can be intrusive. One option is to use acrylic filler and smooth it out as much as possible.

Integrating Roads into Terrain Panels

Flexible acrylic sealant can be used to create integral unmade roads or tracks on high density foam, as was the case with a terrain panel system that I built for the Minehead Wargames Club. To create my integral road I first used a small block sander to create a slightly recessed area in the terrain panel (Figure 187). I could have stopped at that point and coated the recessed area with PVA, followed by a sprinkling of fine sand, but I wanted to create a particular effect, so I filled the recess with brown flexible acrylic sealant, and used a broken plastic comb to rough up the surface of the road before the sealant dried (Figure 188). Once the sealant had completely dried, I gave the road a pale yellow drybrush to create a dusty effect.

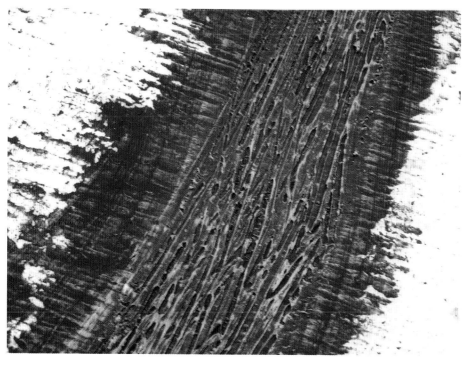

Figure 188:
A close up of the road surface.

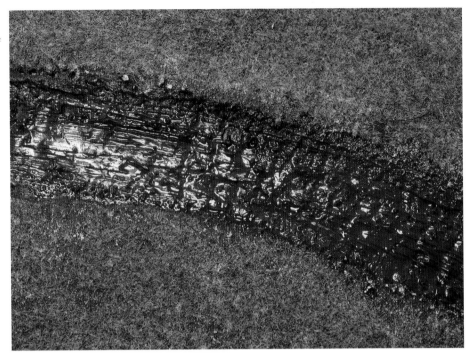

Once the surrounding terrain has been painted, it enhances the effect if you brush a line of PVA glue along the sides of the road and apply static grass or a few random stones (Figure 189). If the road or track is relatively unused, you can run a line of grass along the crown of the road too. I wanted to suggest an unmade up road with water in the ruts, so I painted thinned black into the ruts and once dry, went over the water with gloss varnish.

For tarmac roads, my method is to cut wet-and-dry paper to size and glue it straight onto the terrain tile. Bear in mind that wet-and-dry is generally only available in A4 sized sheets which means that creating bends without any joins is difficult unless the roads are particularly narrow. An alternative material is the belt used on belt sanders, which can be bought in a range of widths from 1cm to 15cm and in lengths from 53cm to 122cm. Both these materials are available in different grades: the lower the number such as 40 or 60, the coarser the surface. The smaller the scale of figures or vehicles that will be using your tarmac roads, the finer should be the grade of material. This material may not be readily available in black and so will need painting and possibly drybrushing to bring out the texture.

Creating Separate Roads

There are many different techniques for making separate roads, starting with cutting a strip of brown felt or fleece and laying it on top of a terrain mat, as was the case with *Langensalza* presented by Keith Flint (Figure 190).

Figure 190:
Felt roads in
Langensalza.
(*Keith Flint*)

If you've not tried it, don't knock it: it's quick and easy. And remember, you don't need to create complicated sculpted terrain in order to have a good game. For most wargamers, a good game is one in which everyone enjoys themselves: it's not about terrain or winning at all costs, it's about having fun. Ultimately we all just find the approach that suits us and which combines the right look with, in my case, cheapness and ease of construction.

The most important consideration when deciding your road building technique is whether or not you want your roads to be rigid or flexible. Rigid roads tend to be easier to make than flexible ones, so lets consider a couple of rigid road options first.

Unmade Roads and Tarmac Roads

I've grouped these distinct types of roads together because they follow the same construction process. In both cases I cut vinyl floor tiles to the size of my roads, including T-junctions and crossroads as necessary.

For my unmade roads I either coat the underside of the tile with PVA glue and sprinkle on fine sand, or apply a layer of flexible acrylic sealant which I texture to create the required effect: perhaps cart wheels, tyres or tank tracks depending on whether I want to make the roads period specific or not (Figures 191–192). The surface is then painted to suit the general locality, and static grass is applied if required.

For tarmac roads, I again start with a vinyl floor tile but apply either wet-and-dry paper or belt sander refills (sprayed matt black) to the adhesive

Figure 191:
An unmade road
made with flexible
sealant coating.

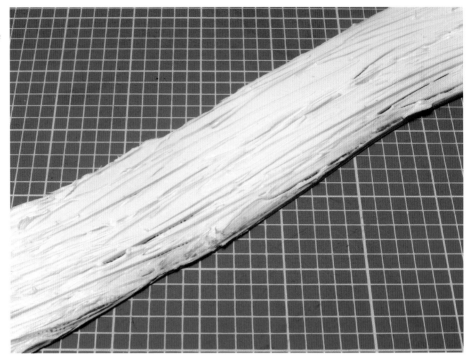

Figure 192:
A completed
section of unmade
road.

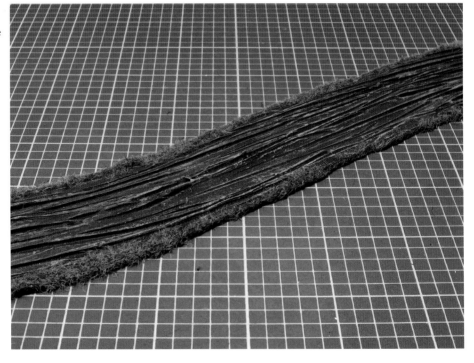

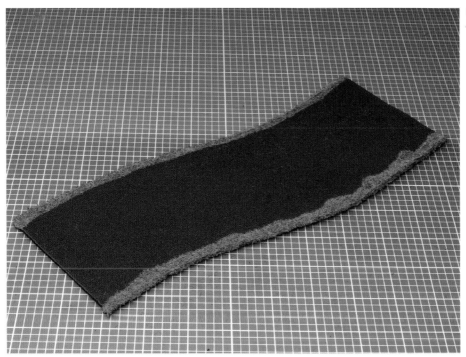

surface (Figure 193). I always prefer to add a verge of some sort along the edges of my roads to help make the transition from the road to the surrounding ground more gentle or subtle. And there's another useful benefit if you pick floor tiles that are blue or green, and don't make your texturing too thick: then on one side you'll have a road and on the other a river!

COBBLED ROADS

Cobbles are irregularly shaped stones laid to form paths or roads. However, if the surface consists of regular shaped stones primarily laid flat, then they are known as setts.

If you want to create a cobbled street or one using setts, the easiest method is to use embossed wallpaper with a suitable pattern, gluing it to appropriately cut sections of floor tiles and painting accordingly. I usually give the paper a matt black undercoat followed by a mid grey drybrush and then pick out individual cobbles in a much lighter grey and sometimes add static grass between some of the cobbles (Figure 194).

151

Figure 194:
A cobbled road piece.

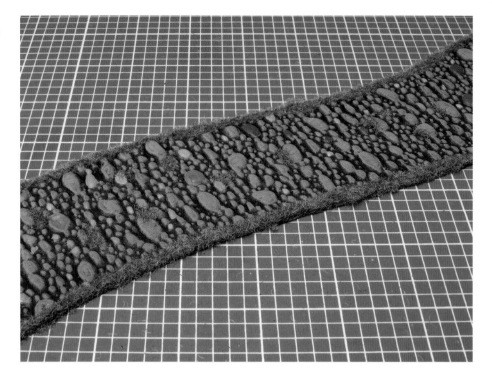

VILLAGE SQUARE

You can make your village square following the same technique as for cobbled roads, but another option is to buy vinyl floor tiles with suitable patterns on them to save you a great deal of time (Figure 195). And if you prefer, you can simply cut these tiles into strips to create road sections. One word of advice though, particularly if buying tiles online: the colours can vary between batches, so if possible try to anticipate your likely future needs and buy all your tiles at the same time so that they will match each other. This is another one of those lessons that I learned the hard way.

Creating Flexible Roads

Most methods for creating flexible roads involve coating a suitable material with flexible sealant, which is then textured and painted. The material used varies from anti-weed matting to pond liner; I tend to use thick butyl rubber, which is used for damp courses. The following technique explains the general process, but before picking up your scalpel blade and getting stuck in, this is one of those happy accident projects to which I referred earlier in the book, so it's worth reading through the technique first to see the conclusion.

The first step is to decide on the length and shape of your roads and cut them from butyl rubber. The butyl rubber is then coated with flexible sealant. You can buy it in various shades of brown, which can save some

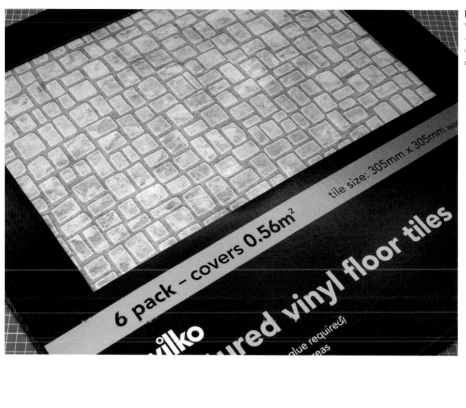

Figure 195:
Vinyl floor tiles
– an alternative
way to represent
cobbles.

Figure 196:
A sanded road
painted with Exotic
Spice 2.

Figure 197:
Roads after the
first drybrush.

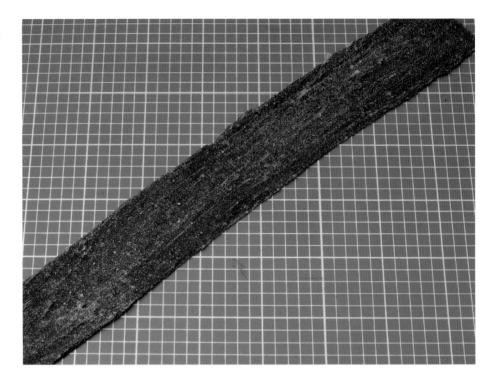

Figure 198:
Peeling the road.

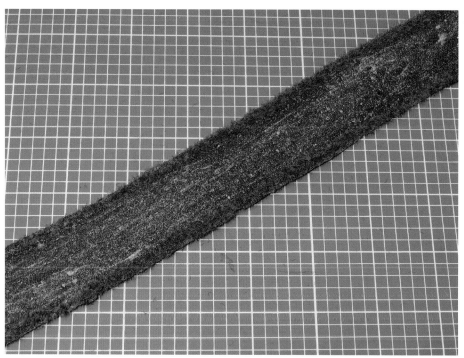

Figure 199:
The finished
flexible road.

Figure 200:
Why make one
road when you can
make more?

time. Unfortunately at the time of making these roads for this book, my local DIY store only had the white variety. Whichever product you use, make sure that it will take paint. Spread the sealant as thinly and evenly as possible and leave it to dry thoroughly.

Brush PVA glue onto the sealant, and sieve on fine sand (Figure 196). Once the PVA is dried – I'd leave it overnight, at the least – paint the sanded surface with your chosen base colour. I used Dulux Exotic Spice 2. Drybrush the surface with Dulux Eastern Spice 2 (Figure 197).

And this is where things got weird! Having left my flexible roads overnight to dry, I picked up one section the following day to examine it. Shock! Horror! The sealant had slightly separated from the butyl rubber. I was about to bin the lot when I had a thought, and I carefully pulled the sealant further … it peeled cleanly away and I finished up with a length of thin, flexible road (Figure 198). It wasn't the way I expected the technique to work, but after I'd applied PVA glue to the edges of the road sections and added some static grass I found myself with some very nice flexible roads (Figure 199). And remember that when making roads, or any scenery, it's always more time, and cost-effective, to make as many different pieces as possible (Figure 200).

16

BRIDGES

Bridges come in all shapes and sizes. The only constraints are that they are must be long enough to span the gap they cross, wide enough to allow appropriate sized vehicles over them and strong enough to take the weight. Bridges for wargaming have to follow the same principles (Figure 201).

PROJECT 16: A Wooden Bridge

This bridge is intended to be crossable by pedestrians or possibly horsemen or a light cart, so it has no supports beneath it.

MATERIALS
- Balsa stripwood
- Balsa sheet

CONSTRUCTION
Cut two lengths of balsa as supporting beams, long enough to span the gap and rest on both river banks. I've used rectangular section balsa rather than

Figure 201:
Robin Hood and Little John meet on the bridge in *A King's Ransom.* (*The Minehead Wargames Club*)

Figure 202:
The common
directions in which
different profile
wood most readily
bends.

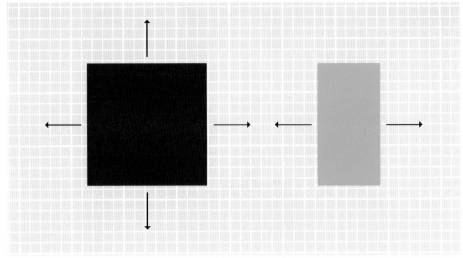

square for the supporting beams because I find it has a tendency to warp less (Figure 202).

Cut planks from sheet balsa and glue them into position (Figure 203). The bridge looks best if the planks overlap the supports. If you're in a hurry, you can use superglue, but ideally I recommend using adhesives specifically formulated for the material in use.

Figure 203:
A simple wooden
bridge over a TSS
terrain tile.

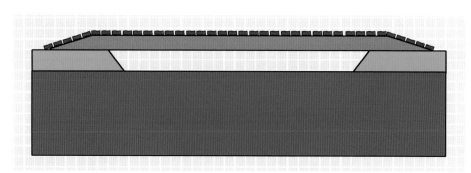

Figure 204:
Profile plan to
create a bridge
with sloping ends.

The supports have the effect of raising the level of the planks. I don't have a problem with this because it brings the planks up to the level of my roads. If you have roads built into your terrain and so don't want the bridge to be raised, you need to give the supporting beams a taper at each end (Figure 204).

For a bit more variation, you can add handrails (Figure 205). Simply cut selected planks flush with the outside edges of the supports so that you can glue uprights into position and finally add handrails.

Unless representing very recently cut timber, I follow the same procedure for painting wood, namely a black undercoat, followed by successively lighter grey drybrushing. For new wood, which tends to feature rarely in my models, I usually undercoat with a pale cream, followed by a lighter drybrush on the upper surfaces that catch the light. But as ever, there is no substitute for taking reference photographs of the real thing.

Figure 205:
A bridge with
handrails.

PROJECT 17: A Different Wooden Bridge

Unlike the previous wooden bridge, which just rested on both river banks, I wanted this one to look more solid with its own supports. Since this bridge was to be used with canal or docklands terrain, it had to fit precisely between perpendicular walls. How I built the docklands themselves is covered in Chapter Six.

MATERIAL
- Balsa stripwood
- Balsa sheet

CONSTRUCTION
The basic design featured a pair of uprights with two supporting beams onto which wooden planks were fixed. To ensure a strong joint between uprights and beams, I drilled a hole so that each beam could be pinned to the cross beam (Figure 206). For accuracy it's a good idea to drill the holes for both beams at the same time.

A cross beam was pinned to the uprights and two angled supports were glued into place. Cut two short beams, and glue them into position. Add two angled supports between the short beams and the adjacent uprights (Figures 207–208). Make the other side assembly and glue it into place, along with the angled supports (Figure 209).

Figure 206:
Drilling uprights to support cross beams.

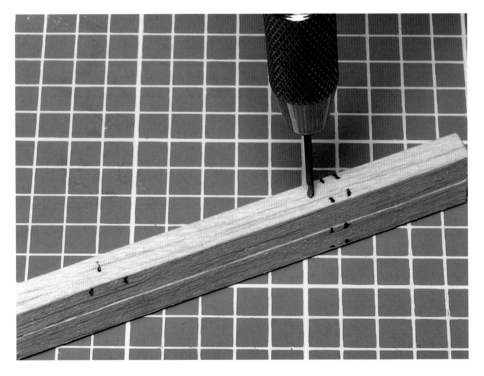

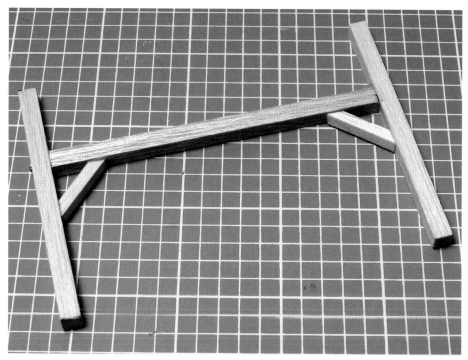

Figure 207:
Spanning beams with supports added.

Figure 208:
Cross beams with supports added.

Figure 209:
A completed frame assembly.

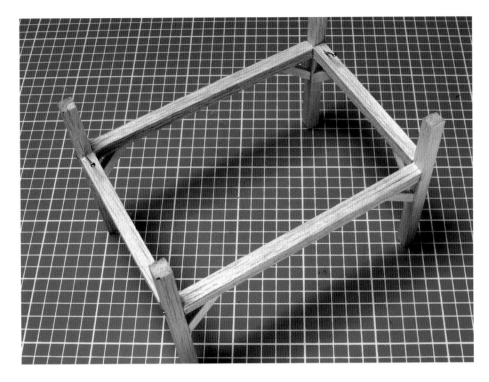

Figure 210:
The unpainted bridge.

Figure 211:
A variation on the wooden bridge.

Figure 212:
The finished bridge positioned in the docklands.

Cut the planks to size and glue them across the supporting beams. Note that the planks between the uprights are trimmed shorter to fit (Figure 210). Another simple variation is to cut the uprights flush with the top edge of the cross beams and run the planks at each end to the full width of the bridge (Figure 211).

Finally the bridge was given a black undercoat, followed by a grey drybrush (Figure 212). I find Dulux Flint works well, but take a look in your local DIY store: most of them have colour charts and cards to enable you to pick the range of colours that suit you the best.

PROJECT 18: Pons Sublicius

This bridge model is based upon the *Pons Sublicius:* the bridge across the Tiber defended by Publius Horatius Cocles against the Etruscans in 508 BC. The bridge is built in two stages: the bridge itself, and the supports. Unsurprisingly there isn't much (any) reference material specific to *Pons Sublicius* – all I could find was a Wikipedia article – so it was a case of coming up with a design that looked right, but under the circumstances it was unlikely that anyone could say with any real authority that my representation was incorrect.

MATERIALS
- Balsa stripwood
- Balsa sheet

CONSTRUCTION
Cut two beams, long enough to span your river allowing about 2.5cm overlap at each end. I always use rectangular section balsa for my spans to reduce the likelihood of them bending (Figure 213). This is a long bridge and needs a series of additional cross beams. To ensure accurate right angle joints I called upon my ready supply of Lego bricks, and pinned each beam in place as well as gluing … it's the only way to be sure (Figure 214).

The number of cross beams depends on the length of your bridge, but I always err on the side of caution and would rather use too many than too few. Once all of the cross beams are in position, add the other spanning beam and leave the assembly to dry thoroughly (Figure 215). Plank the bridge by cutting planks out from sheet balsa (Figure 216). The sides of the bridge consist of a series of open frames. They may look complicated but if you study the diagrammatic view (Figure 217) and the follow the step-by-step photographs they are straightforward to make if you take your time!

The diagonal pieces within each frame have to overlap each other, which means that they must be no more than half the thickness of the outer frames. For example, if the outer frames are 0.4cm thick, the inner diagonal pieces must be no more than 0.2cm thick. Create your first outer frame by pinning and gluing together the four sides. Each frame is divided into two so add the central upright (Figures 218–219).

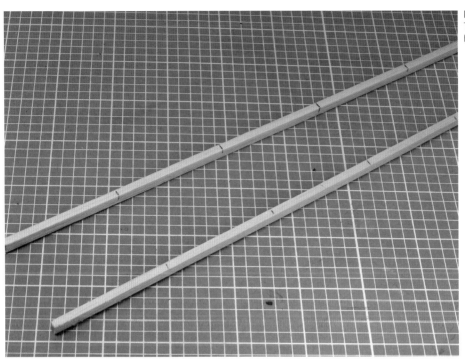

Figure 213:
The spanning
beams.

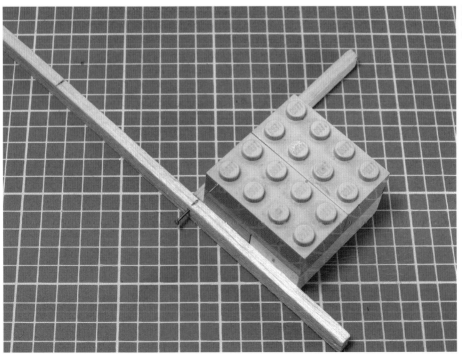

Figure 214.
Fitting the first
cross beam.

Figure 215:
The completed
sub-frame.

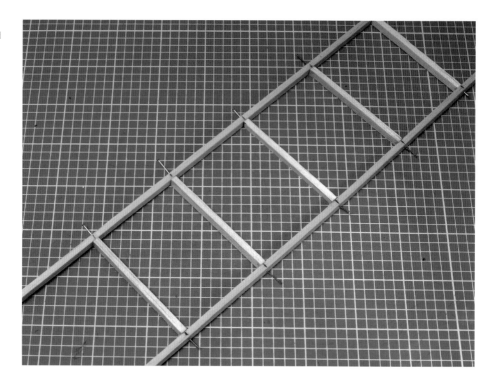

Figure 216:
The basic planked
bridge.

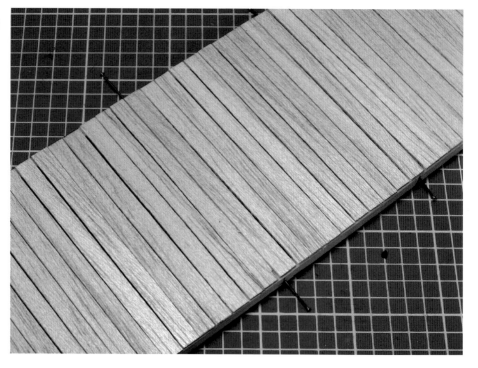

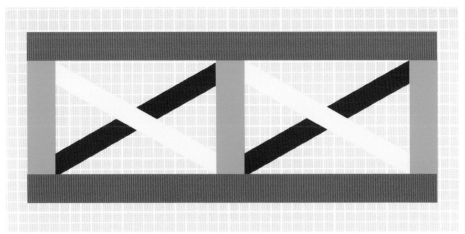

Figure 217:
Diagrammatic view
of a section of side
panels.

The next stage is adding the diagonals which must fit flush inside the outer frame and which are half the thickness of the outer frames (Figure 220). Fit the diagonals on one side of the frame first. Turn the frame over and repeat the process (Figure 221).

Once you have made all the frames, glue the first one in position (Figure 222). I used Lego bricks to keep the frame upright while the glue dried. Glue the remaining frames into position to complete the basic bridge (Figure 223).

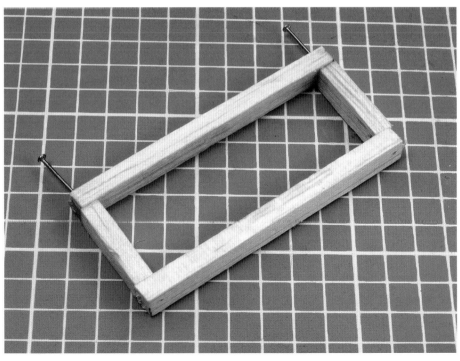

Figure 218:
The outer frame:
stage 1.

Figure 219:
The outer frame:
stage 2.

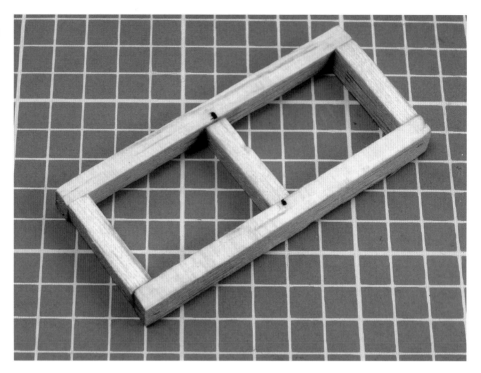

Figure 220:
Fitting the first
diagonals.

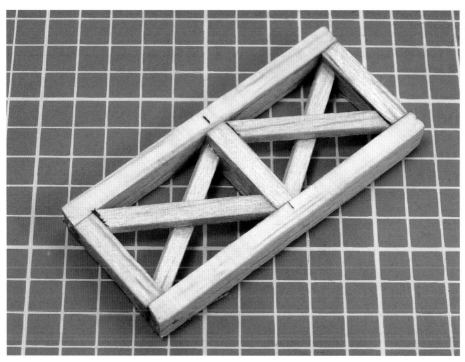

Figure 221:
A completed frame.

Figure 222:
The first frame is glued into position.

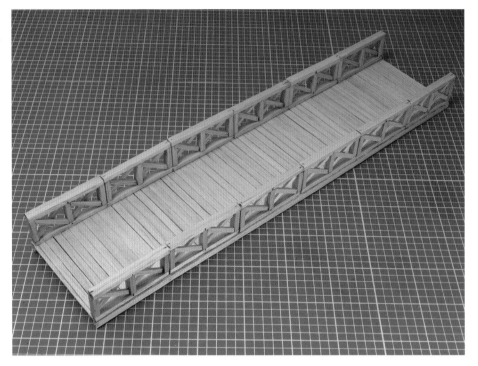

You could stop at this stage, because the bridge will now rest on the opposite river banks and span any depth of river. However, I wanted to go a few steps further by adding supports to the bridge. After all, it was originally built to carry the massed legions of Republican Rome! If you decide to add supports, bear in mind that a bridge without supports will fit any terrain system, whereas one with supports may have limited usability. One other option, depending on the height of your river banks above the water level could be to slide pontoons beneath the bridge.

Assuming you want to add supports, cut four lengths of balsa long enough to be flush with the top of the sides of the bridge and to rest on your river, and glue them into position (Figure 224). Add cross pieces between the supports (Figure 225).

Never one to do things by halves, I decided that the overall appearance of the bridge would be further enhanced if I added additional supporting struts (Figure 226). At this point, I thought that my representation of *Pons Sublicius* looked pretty reasonable (Figure 227).

Remember what I said about the addition of supports potentially limiting the usage of the bridge? Well I unexpectedly found myself having to fit my bridge over a deeper river! If you find yourself in a similar predicament, do not despair, there's an easy solution: I call them 'boots' (Figure 228).

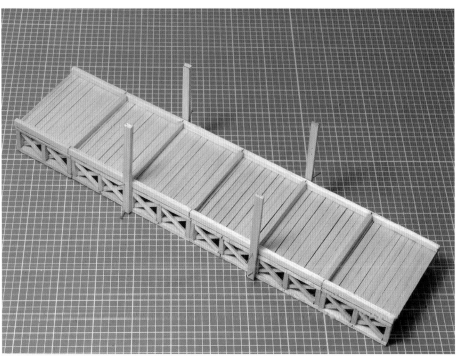

Figure 224:
The main bridge supports.

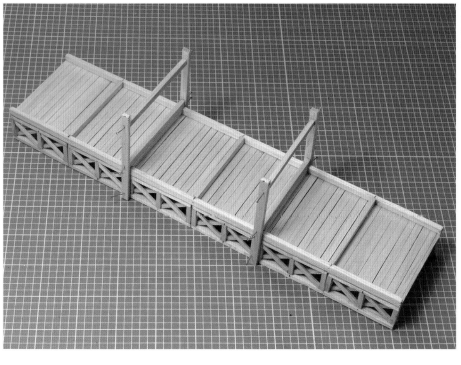

Figure 225:
Cross pieces added to the supports.

Figure 226:
Supports with
bracing pieces
added.

Figure 227:
The finished
bridge? Well
almost!

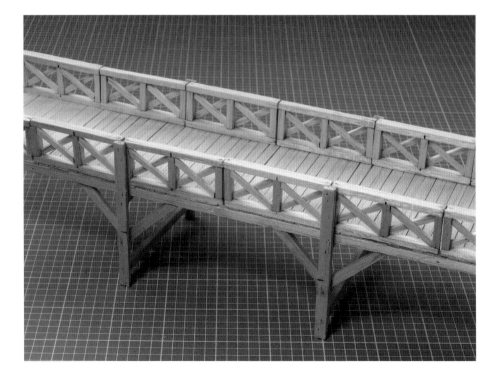

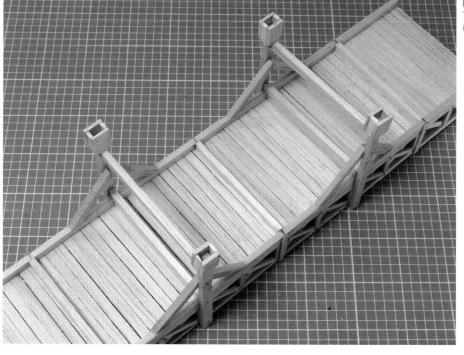

Figure 230:
The painted bridge ready for Publius Horatius Cocles to take his place.

Just make a number of open boxes into which the supports can fit. The boots just slide over the bridge supports so that you can make your bridge fit virtually any height of river bank (Figure 229).

I paint aged unpainted or untreated wood in the same way: a black undercoat followed by a drybrush of a mid tone grey, followed by a highlight of pale grey. Sometimes, depending on the subject, I might add some random green streaks to simulate moss or mildew. It's also possible to use wood stain to colour wood, but there can be problems with this. Wood stain tends to be transparent, which means that pencil or pen marks will show up. Also in areas where glue has spread onto the surface of the wood, it won't absorb as much, if any, of the stain, causing potentially unsightly patches.

The decision that I had to make with my *Pons Sublicius* was whether the wood, which in real life would have had to carry significant loads, would have been allowed to age and potentially weaken the structure. I decided not, and therefore painted the wood using a thinned pale cream to give the impression of relatively new timber that had been well maintained (Figure 230).

REFERENCES

Unsurprisingly with a wooden bridge that was built over 2,500 years ago, there isn't much contemporary reference material to be found. It's a case therefore of creating a structure that follows the established style of Roman bridges and which looks right. However, I did find the following publication, which contained a useful artist's impression of a Roman bridge that looked the part.

Connolly, P., *Tiberius Claudius Maximus: The Legionary* (Oxford University Press, 1988)

17

DEFENCES

Defences can take many forms, from a simple wall to a rampart topped by a palisade or even a stone curtain wall for a medieval castle. Unfortunately, in a book of this size it's not possible to include everything, so this chapter will just demonstrate how to construct some simple defences of the type that an army could carry with it, or easily build when needed.

PROJECT 19: Chevaux-de-frise

'Chevaux-de-frise' is the plural of cheval-de-frise, which derives from the French for 'horse of the Friesians'. Apparently the Friesians didn't have any cavalry so they invented a defence against them; they obviously worked because they've been used for hundreds of years, from medieval times, the American Civil War to the Second World War (Figure 231). Sometimes they were used en masse to form a defensive line, other times to act as a simple movable barricade on a road.

Figure 231: Chevaux-de-frise in the American Civil War.

MATERIALS

- Square section balsa
- Cocktail sticks, toothpicks or wire

CONSTRUCTION

Construction of the chevaux-de-frise is very simple: a square or round section beam is pierced by stakes of wood or metal, each one at 90° to the adjacent one (Figure 232).

Figure 232:
Schematic cross-section of the main beam.

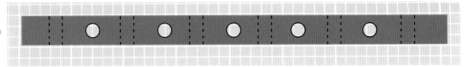

Take a length of square section balsa and cut it to the appropriate length. The size of the balsa beam will depend on the scale of your chevaux-de-frise. Remember that you will need to drill holes through the main beam for the spikes, so you might find that the best approach is to determine the thickness of the spikes first, and then choose a beam with a large enough cross-section to allow you to drill through it, leaving sufficient space around the holes so that you don't risk splitting the beam when you push them through.

To decide on the length for your spikes you need to bear in mind that the beam needs to sit halfway up the spike, and in most cases needs to be somewhere between the waist and shoulder height of your figures.

Figure 233:
Painted chevaux-de-frise.

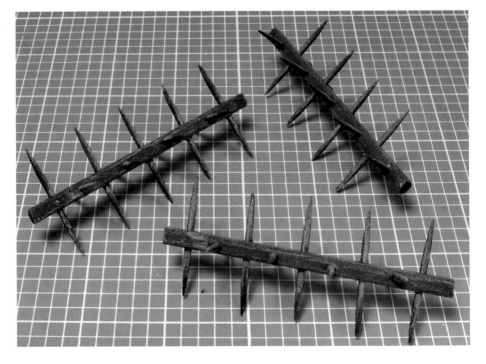

The material for the spikes depends on the scale of your chevaux-de-frise. Cocktail sticks or toothpicks work well for most scales, but if you are intending to make very small scale examples you're likely to have to use wire instead. I suggest piano wire because it doesn't bend.

Cut your spikes to length and push them through the drilled holes. Chevaux-de-frise could be all wood, all metal or a mixture of both with a wooden beam and metal spikes, so how you paint yours is up to you. I'd standardise on a black undercoat, and then drybrush with grey for wood, gunmetal for metal (Figure 233), and I doubt very much that any rivet counter will point out that 'in such-and-such a year they would have been made in whatever.' If they do ... politely direct them towards the door.

PROJECT 20: An Artillery Defensive Position

Stronger defensive works for longer sieges were created from earth mounds that might be topped with gabions, fascines or sandbags. Inside this defensive area, wooden planks were laid to provide a floor on which cannon and artillerymen could stand (Figure 234).

MATERIALS
- High density foam
- Balsa, thick card

Figure 234:
A pair of artillery positions.

Figure 235:
It helps to set out your cannons and crew before deciding on the size of your earthworks.

Figure 236:
A plan of a suggested artillery position.

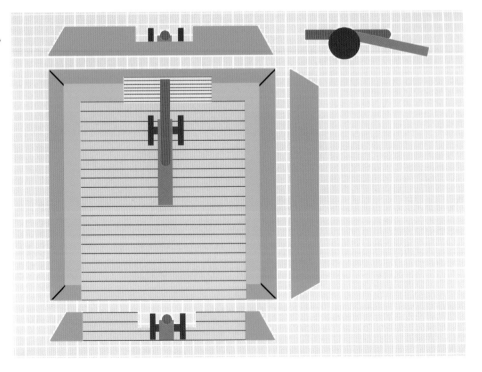

CONSTRUCTION

Determining the size of your earthwork really depends on the size and number of cannons you intend to place within it, as well as the number of crew. I find it's visually helpful to set these elements out onto a piece of card (Figure 235).

My plan suggests a possible layout for a defensive position, but you can adjust the shape, size and proportions to accommodate the number of cannons and crew (Figure 236). Once you have determined the overall dimensions for your defensive position, cut out the shape from high density foam and mark out the top of the earthworks to provide a guide to cutting the angled front and sides (Figure 237).

Carefully cut the angled front and sides as well as the aperture for the cannon (Figure 238). A hot wire cutter makes this process easier and less messy, but take care to use it in a well-ventilated area.

The card on which you planned the interior of your earthworks comes in useful now and becomes the floor onto which you can add the planking made from balsa strips (Figure 239). Glue the floor in place and cut planks from balsa to line the inner walls and the aperture for the cannon barrel (Figure 240). Cut some thin strips of balsa for the uprights that help to hold the horizontal planks in position, and glue them in place (Figure 241).

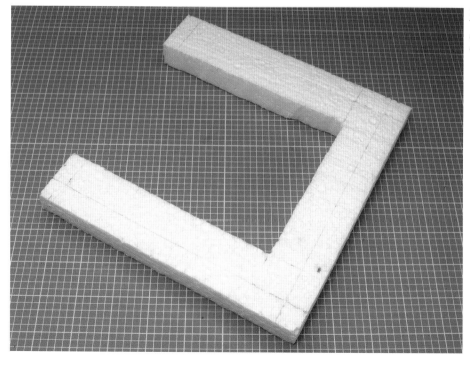

Figure 237:
The rough cut artillery earthworks.

Figure 238:
The earthworks are starting to look like earthworks!

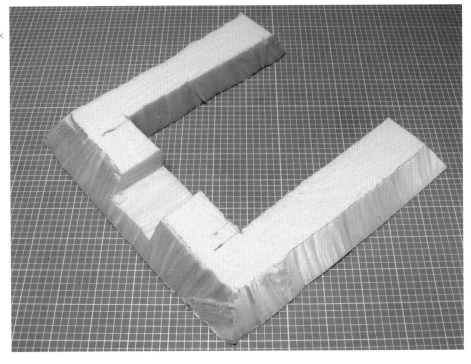

Figure 239:
The inner planked area.

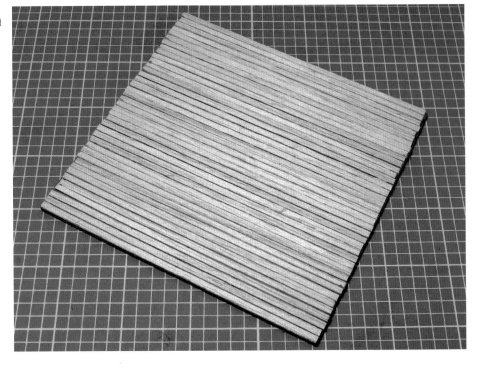

Figure 240:
The earthworks
based and the
floor in position.

Figure 241:
The vertical
supporting pieces
in place.

At this point, you might feel the need to run a light coat of filler over the outer slopes of the earthwork. The best way to obtain a smooth finish is to lightly wet a coffee stirrer or a lolly stick and use it to smooth the filler, but these types of defences were often not built to particularly high standards, so you can leave the surface irregular if you prefer. Once the filler has completely dried, the next stage is texturing the earthworks by applying PVA glue to the earth areas and sprinkling on fine sand. It can enhance the overall effect if you glue some small pieces of gravel or pebbles around the base of the earthwork too.

The earthworks would have been constructed from material found nearby, so your model should be painted to match your terrain. My suggestion is to paint the earthworks a dark brown with a drybrush of lighter brown. There would have probably been some grass in amongst the material used, so I applied small patches of static grass randomly on the earth, but this should be done sparingly unless the defensive position has been in place for long enough for larger areas of grass to have become established.

As for the wood, you've got several choices. It can be weathered and aged timber, or freshly cut. If the former I apply a black undercoat followed by a grey drybrush (Figure 242); if the latter, I generally paint the wood with a very thinned light cream: I use Dulux Golden Umber 3. You could also use wood stain or varnish, but be warned that wood stain is transparent so any marks on the balsa will show through the stain.

Figure 242: The painted earthworks.

182

PROJECT 21: A Late Antiquity Hill Fort

Whilst browsing through two of my Osprey Fortress books (*Roman Legionary Fortresses 27BC–AD378* and *British Forts in the Age of Arthur*), I realised that with a little artistic licence it would be possible to create the gatehouse, rampart and palisade of a fort that could be used across a period of more than five hundred years, because generally the design of the fortifications themselves didn't alter very much. It was the buildings inside that placed the fort historically, whilst the materials used in the fort's construction positioned it geographically.

When the Roman army was on campaign, their forts tended to be temporary structures, but once it became an army of occupation they became more permanent. Roman forts were usually built on flat or prepared areas of ground, and were generally rectangular or square in shape, because if there were any obstructions in the way the Romans flattened them.

By contrast, many British defences were hill forts, the outer walls of which followed the shape of the hilltop. From a modelmaking viewpoint, and at the risk of stating the obvious, the only difference between a fort and a hill fort is that the latter was, well … on a hill. My reason for sharing this piece of mind-shattering information is that if you decide to build your fort separate from terrain, you will have the option of using it both as a hill fort and as a fort positioned on the flat (Figure 243). As you will probably already have

Figure 243:
Waiting for the enemy to appear at the hill fort.

worked out, I always try to get value for money from anything I build, so the wider the period over which I can reasonably use a model, the more I like it.

I have loosely based this model around the reconstructions of South Cadbury in Somerset, but with a certain amount of artistic license where this made the design and construction easier. South Cadbury was a hill fort, so the ramparts conformed to the shape of the hill and I have built my ramparts to follow a similarly varied shape. If you want to build a Roman fort, just make straight ramparts with right angled corners.

I didn't want to construct the entire fort because it would have occupied too much space on my wargame table, so instead I built a section of rampart with a gatehouse to run across one end; by following the same techniques, you could make the fort as large as you wished. To further enhance this particular model you can find how to make a Saxon Great Hall and some generic village buildings in Chapter Eighteen.

MATERIALS
- Balsa
- High density foam
- Cocktail sticks
- Stone effect textured wallpaper

It is clear from my reference sources that the stone facing of the ramparts was created using dressed stone, which was relatively regular in shape. You can create this effect by etching the pattern into the high density foam or by coating the ramparts with DAS Pronto air-drying, but as I wasn't attempting to construct a precise replica of South Cadbury as envisaged by archaeologists, I took the easy option and used some textured wallpaper.

CONSTRUCTION
The first step is to determine the size of the ramparts and gatehouse. I find that the best method is to relate its dimensions to the size of a figure; for example, the ramparts need to be high enough to force infantry to use ladders to climb over, and the palisade along the top needs to be high enough to provide shelter for defenders (albeit with strategically placed gaps through which they can fling spears or shoot arrows). As for the gatehouse it must be at least as high as the top of the palisade. The floors must be far enough apart so that a based figure can stand inside without banging their head, and the gateway needs to be high enough and wide enough for a small wagon to pass through (Figure 244).

Since the construction of this model is relatively complicated, I have separated it into two distinct areas:

- The ramparts topped with palisade
- The gatehouse

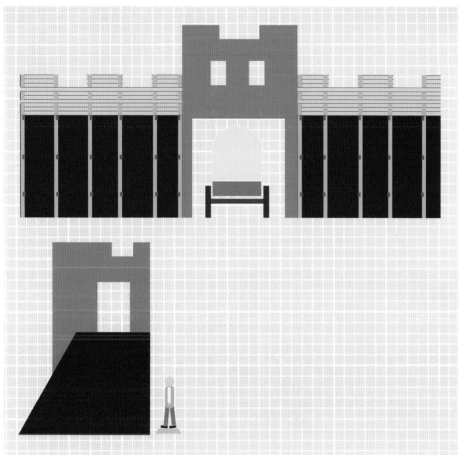

Figure 244:
Create your plans
based upon the
dimensions of
a wagon and a
figure.

Ramparts and Palisade

I decided that my fort would have the general look of a hill fort with ramparts that were angled to each other as if following the line of a hilltop.

The first step was to create my rampart sections. The best method is to build them in blocks without worrying about the rear slope, so that you can concentrate on the angles at which they meet each other. When you're planning these sections, give some thought to where you intend to store the fort when not in use. I'd even go so far to suggest that you buy your storage boxes first and then cut the rampart sections so that they will fit the box! Once you're happy with the ramparts in their basic form, make a template so that the ends of each section will match up (Figure 245).

Use your template to mark out the profile on the end faces of each section, and then cut the angled rear slope of each section using either a saw or a hot wire cutter. The latter makes less mess, but can use up batteries very quickly, so if you have a lot of cutting and shaping to do make sure you have some spare batteries.

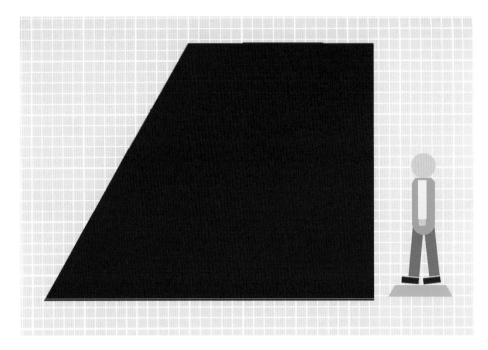

If you decide to fix several of your wall sections together, my method is to spread No More Nails or similar instant grab adhesive onto both ends of adjacent wall sections, and then slide them together whilst they are resting on a flat surface. It helps to hold the sections together if you push cocktail sticks through adjacent sections (Figure 246). Once the glued sections have dried thoroughly, trim off any exposed stick ends, making sure that there is nothing protruding above the surface level.

The ramparts were made from a mix of local stone and earth with the front faced with larger stones, and this is the effect that I wanted to create with my model. It is possible to etch the stonework into the front surface of the high density foam or you can coat the front surface of the ramparts with air-drying clay or Milliput, and engrave the pattern of the stonework into the surface before it dries, but I decided to take the easy option and used textured wallpaper instead (Figure 247).

In the real world, the ramparts were constructed by first building a wooden framework that was then filled with stones and compacted earth. The front uprights were notched to take the horizontal beams, and also extended upwards to support the horizontal planks that protected the troops defending the battlements. The schematic (Figure 248) shows how the horizontal beams notch into the front uprights.

You're going to need quite a few of these uprights. Exactly how many will depend on the configuration of the crenellations along the upper edge of the battlements. As a guide, I used the height of a based foot figure as the approximate distance between the crenellations.

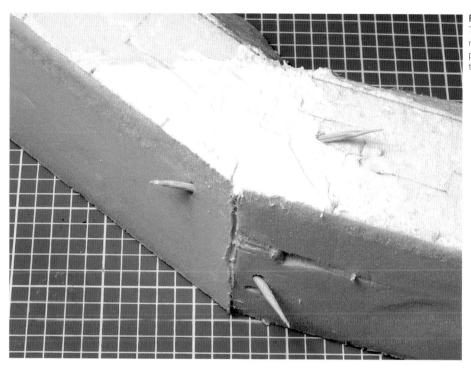

Figure 246:
Two adjacent
rampart sections
pinned and glued
together.

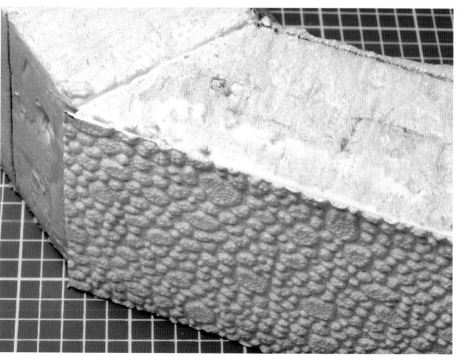

Figure 247:
Textured wallpaper
glued into position.

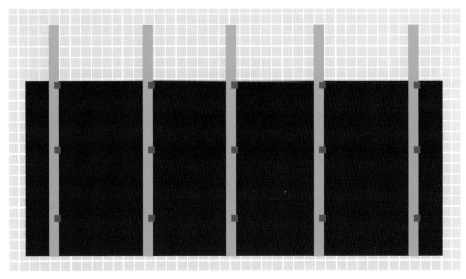

Figure 248:
How to notch the front uprights to take the horizontal beams.

Cut out your uprights (Figure 249); based upon my experiences, make more than you need because it's quite easy to break them. Carefully mark out the locations for these notched uprights and glue them into position, until you have completed the section (Figure 250).

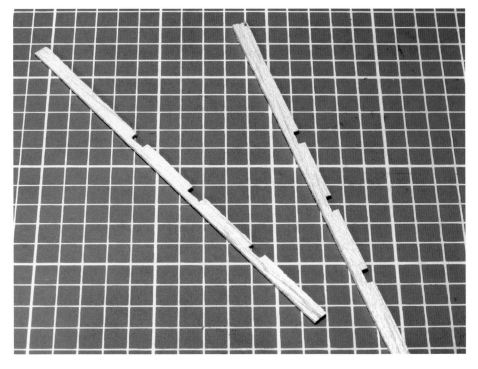

Figure 249:
The notched rampart uprights.

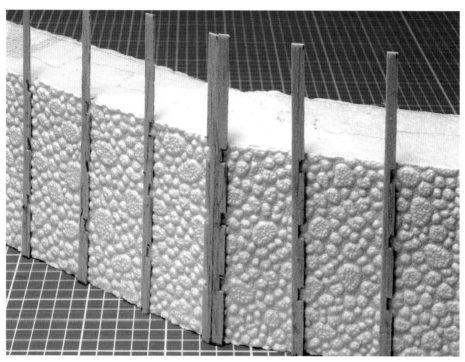

Figure 250:
The rampart uprights glued in place.

Figure 251:
The front of wall with horizontal beam ends.

The framework that formed the basis of the rampart featured horizontal beams (Figure 251). To suggest these, cut short lengths of square section balsa and glue them into the notches on the uprights. With the uprights glued in position, the next step is to add the wooden walkway using strips of thin balsa sheet (Figure 252).

The uprights need to be thickened up; cut lengths of square section balsa matching the width of the uprights and glue them behind the uprights and to the walkway (Figure 253). To complete the impression of the wooden underframe, make a series of holes in the upper surface of the rampart in line with the uprights and glue short lengths of balsa into them (Figure 254).

Next you need to create the crenellations from lengths of balsa, glued to the uprights with the joins between each section staggered with the one above (Figure 255). Start with the lowest row resting on the beam ends that extend at right angles from the front wall, adding additional rows until you have completed the battlements. For added strength I inserted short lengths of square section balsa between the uprights on the inside of the battlements (Figure 256). With all the main woodwork completed, the next stage is to simulate the earth of the rampart; this is done by painting the rampart with PVA glue and then sprinkling on fine sand (Figure 257).

Figure 252:
The walkway.

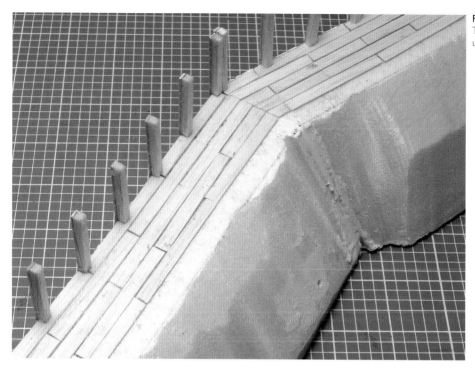

Figure 253:
The strengthened
uprights.

Figure 254:
The walkway rear
supports.

Figure 255:
A view of the completed outer rampart.

Figure 256:
Inner battlement strengtheners.

Figure 257:
The ramparts after
sand has been
sprinkled.

Gatehouse

The gatehouse consists of four uprights joined together by horizontal beams. I set the top surface of the lower horizontal beams to match the top of my ramparts, so that the planked inner floor of the gatehouse would align with the top of the rampart without the need to construct steps (Figure 258).

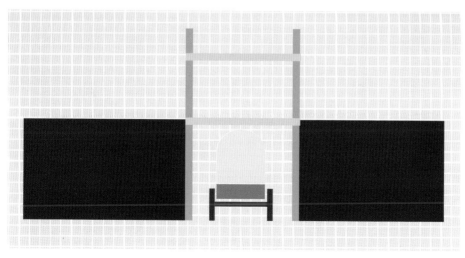

Figure 258:
The floor levels
relative to
ramparts.

Cut out the four uprights. Start by working with one side of vertical beams. To make a strong joint, I use a halving joint (Figure 259). Carefully mark out the uprights and horizontals and cut the halving joint. The halving joint secures the front horizontal beams, but the gatehouse has a pair of assemblies that need to be joined. To add and strengthen the positioning of the short side horizontals I insert a pin through the uprights. Using a pin drill, drill a small hole through the back of the halving joint (Figure 260). Repeat this process on the other joints.

Glue the first short horizontal beam in place, and carefully push a pin through the drilled hole in the back of the joint to hold it in place and strengthen the joint (Figures 261–262). I use Lego bricks to ensure an accurate right angled joint. Make sure that the pin is pushed fully into the joint so that the head is below the surface of the balsa, otherwise the front horizontal beams won't seat properly into the halving joint (Figure 263). Repeat the procedure with the next horizontal. Pin and glue the other upright in place to complete the first assembly. Set this assembly aside to dry and repeat the process to make the other assembly (Figure 264).

Figure 259:
The halving joints.

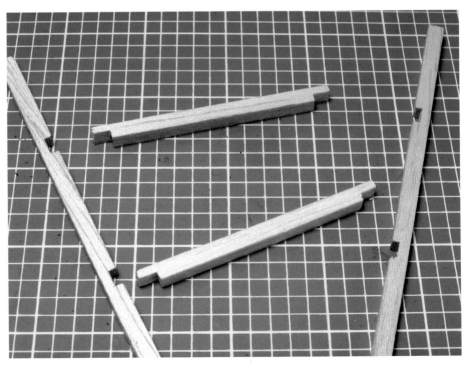

Figure 260:
Drilling through
the uprights to
strengthen the
joints.

Figure 261:
Pinning and gluing
the first horizontal
beam.

Figure 262:
Two pinned and glued joints.

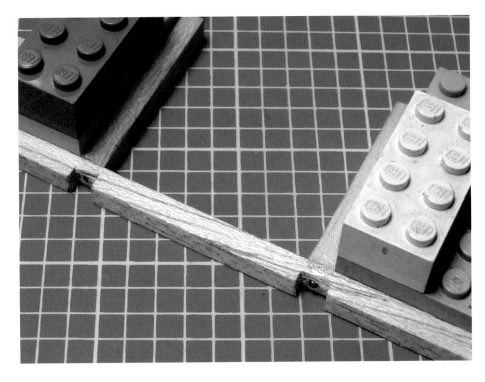

Figure 263:
The completed first assembly.

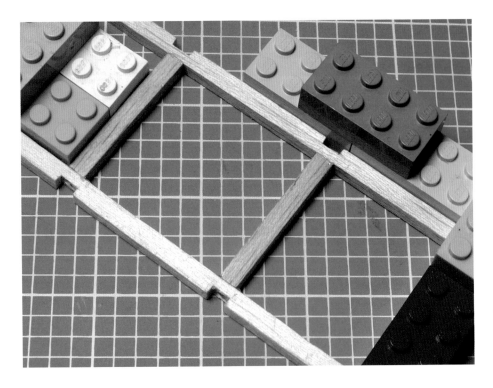

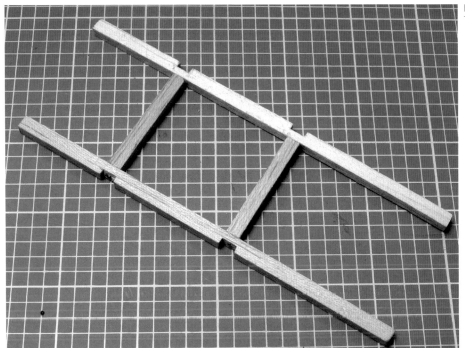

The next stage is to fix the two side assemblies together by gluing the long horizontals in position (Figure 265). Glue the second long horizontal beam in place (Figure 266), and then glue the remaining horizontal beams in place and stand the assembly up using a frame made from Lego to ensure a good right angle (Figure 267).

It's important that the tower framework sits squarely, so I weighted the assembly down to prevent it twisting while the glue dried overnight (Figure 268). I used a telephoto camera lens to provide the weight and a CD case to spread it evenly. Apologies to anyone not a fan of country music; feel free to substitute a music CD of your choice!

The gatehouse is clad with balsa planks (Figure 269). Start by cladding the sides first. Cut square section lengths of balsa for the door uprights and glue them in position (Figure 270). Next cut the verticals to form the sides of the windows on the front face of the gatehouse and glue them in place (Figure 271). Continue cladding the gatehouse (Figure 272). It's much easier to clad up to the approximate location of the window aperture rather than fixing the window horizontal beams in place and then having to precisely cut strips of balsa cladding to fit.

Figure 265:
Gluing the first long horizontal beam into place.

Figure 266:
Gluing the second long horizontal beam into place.

Figure 267:
The completed gatehouse inner frames.

Figure 268:
Weighting down the tower.

Figure 269:
The first cladding.

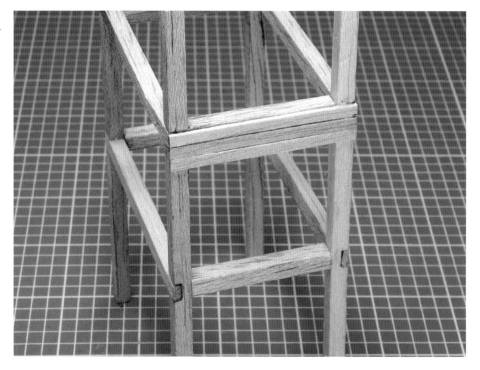

Figure 270:
Adding the door uprights.

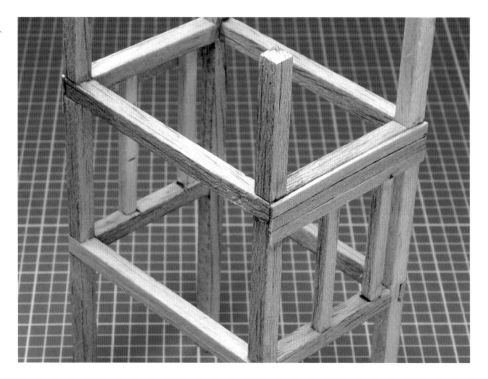

Figure 271:
The window
uprights.

Figure 272:
Adding further
cladding.

Clad around the window apertures (Figure 273), and continue cladding the sides of the gatehouse, and add the horizontal beams above and below both window apertures, and above the door openings. Clad the outside of the building – but not the back – and then cut strips of balsa to make the lower floor and glue them into place (Figures 274–275).

I haven't clad the rear face of the gatehouse because I wanted access to the inside of the tower in order to place figures inside. I made the rear panel removable, by making a rectangular frame that would fit inside the space created by the lower floor, the uprights and the upper horizontal beam (Figure 276). Add the horizontal cladding making sure that it overlaps the edges of the frame to help hold it in position (Figure 277).

The gatehouse has two floors. The lower floor provides access between the rampart sections. The upper floor has a hatch in it through which a ladder allows access between the lower and upper floors (Figure 278).

Create a hatch aperture and floor support and glue it in position. Add the upper floor using balsa planks working around the hatch opening (Figure 279).

You could carry on cladding the gatehouse with horizontal cladding, but as already mentioned, I decided to go for a more interesting option of wattle panels. First I created a series of frames to fit between the uprights (Figures 280–281). The next stage was to drill holes through the horizontal beams to create the framing for the wattle panels. I used jewellery makers' brass head pins because they are fairly rigid but also easy to cut with clippers. The

Figure 273: The cladding around the windows.

Figure 274:
View showing the rear of the front panel.

Figure 275:
The floor added.

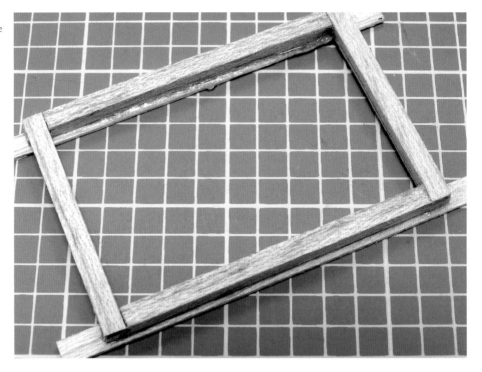

Figure 276:
The frame for the rear wall.

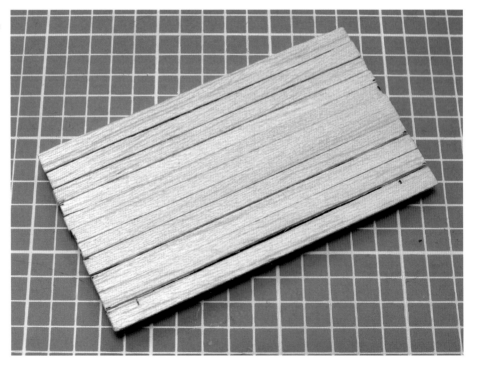

Figure 277:
The rear wall with cladding added.

Figure 278:
The upper hatch
and floor supports.

Figure 279:
The upper floor
added.

Figure 280:
Frames for the
wattle panels.

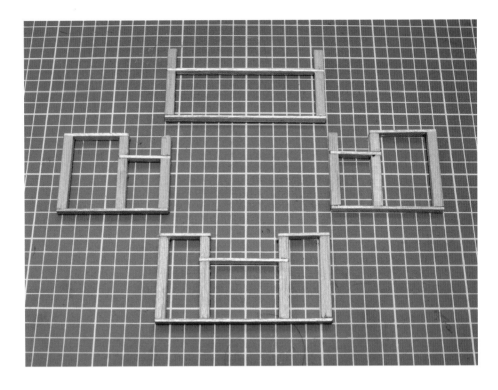

Figure 281:
The vertical beams
added.

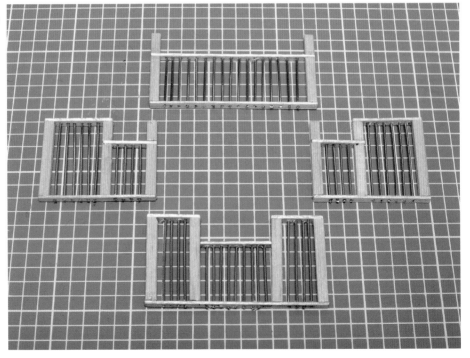

pins are narrower than cocktail sticks, which meant that I could get more of them into the frame to make a more intricate panel.

Thin strips of card are threaded between the wire uprights to simulate the wattle effect (Figure 282); this technique is covered in Chapter Eleven. It can strengthen the wattle if you lightly brush PVA glue over it before you trim off any excess wattle. Each wattle panel was then glued into position and an additional strip of balsa was glued on the upper horizontal surfaces to hide the pin holes (Figure 283).

I decided to integrate a stone floor into the base of the gatehouse to prevent the volume of traffic passing through the gateway from churning up the ground. Cut a piece of balsa sheet that matches the footprint of the four gatehouse uprights, and then glue four edging pieces sized so that the gatehouse uprights will fit around them. Next cut and glue a piece of textured wallpaper to fit inside (Figure 284). The gatehouse uprights are then glued into the spaces in the corners (Figure 285).

The gatehouse needs two pairs of double doors for the outer and inner gatehouse access, and also two side doors to provide access to the ramparts from the gatehouse. I have two methods of making doors: I either cut a piece of balsa sheet to the size of the aperture and score lines on it using an old ballpoint pen to simulate the planks, or glue individual planks to a piece of balsa sheet (Figure 286). Bracing pieces were then glued to the rear of edge door (Figure 287).

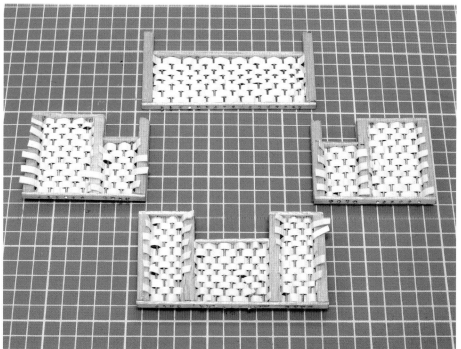

Figure 282:
The woven panels waiting to be trimmed.

Figure 283:
The wattle panels
in place.

Figure 284:
The gateway floor.

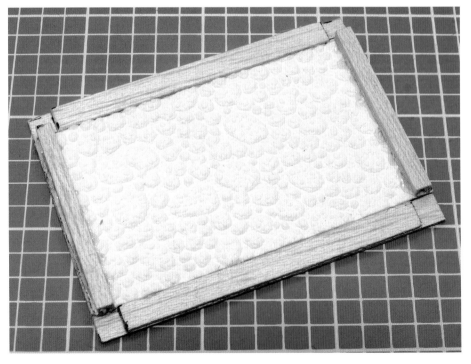

Figure 285:
The gatehouse
uprights in position.

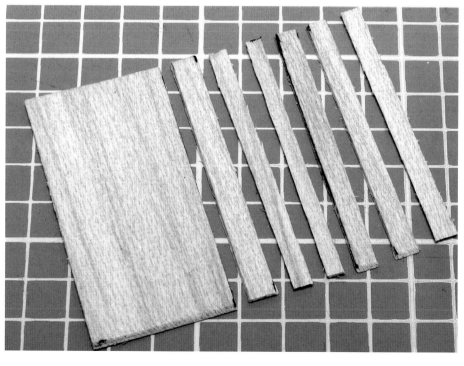

Figure 286:
The door
components.

209

Figure 287:
The doors with cross braces added.

Figure 288:
The ladders.

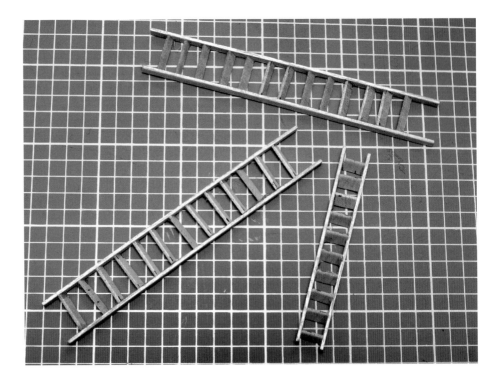

The model needs several ladders: one in the gatehouse for access from the lower floor to the upper floor, and others to enable the defenders to get up onto the ramparts if they are not close to the gatehouse. Construction of the ladders is simply a case of cutting the ladder sides and then gluing the rungs in place (Figure 288).

PAINTING

I wanted the timber of my hill fort to look weathered so I painted it black, drybrushed it with a mid grey and finished off with a very light drybrush of pale grey. You need to be gentle with your drybrushing because balsa wood is relatively fragile.

The exposed earth that makes up the sloping rear of the bank should match the general look of your terrain, which in my case means that I painted PVA glue over the surface and then sprinkled on patches of fine sand (Figure 289). Once dry, I drybrushed the earth with dark brown followed by a pale cream. Finally I applied patches of static grass. Just how much you add, depends on the intended age of the hill fort; a newly created fort would have had scattered areas of grass that were turned over during the construction, but the older the fort, the more grass there would be, particularly on the flat upper surfaces.

Figure 289:
A rear view of the fortifications showing the timber and earth rampart.

Figure 290:
A close-up of the
stonework.

Figure 291:
Age of Arthur
terrain.
(*Crawley Wargames
Club*)

212

Ideally the stonework would be locally sourced. After all, if you've decided to build a fort on top of a hill you don't especially want to be dragging stone from tens of miles away unless it's unavoidable. My technique is to undercoat my stonework with black, highlight it with grey but then mix in a little of the local terrain colour and pick out a few random stones (Figure 290).

The techniques and materials demonstrated in the construction of this model are just one way of creating a generic Romano-British fort. Several years ago I was commissioned by Crawley Wargames Club to build a similar fort for their *Age of Arthur* demonstration game (Figure 291). While following a similar overall design, this model made extensive use of barbeque skewers to clad the tower and to create the palisade instead of balsa planking to create a totally different appearance.

REFERENCES

The period during which, and after, the last Roman forces left Britain is no longer considered to be as 'dark' as it was once thought, and there is an increasing amount of information available on which to base your modelmaking. I found the following publications particularly useful.

Alcock, L., *By South Cadbury, is that Camelot…* (Thames & Hudson, 1972)
Konstam, A., *British Forts in the Age of Arthur* (Osprey, 2008)

18

BUILDINGS

When designing the building projects for inclusion in this book, I tried to balance realism with practicality. Buildings used for wargaming usually get more handling than say, model railway buildings, which in most cases are embedded into a layout where they remain unless the layout goes on display somewhere or the owner moves house. In contrast, wargame buildings are brought out of storage, placed on the terrain, possibly picked up or handled during the game, and then packed away at the end of the battle only to go through the entire process the following week. Unless handled very carefully, it's inevitable that delicate items such as gutters and drainpipes will be accidently damaged over time, so I tend to omit this type of subtle detail in the first place (but by all means feel free to include it to further enhance your own model buildings). For example, constructing a Southern-style mansion was the subject of one of my 'How to…' articles in *Wargames Illustrated*, and wargamer Mark Densham added additional details to personalise it for his collection (Figure 292).

On the subject of preventing damage to buildings, I never design a building without first considering the box in which it will ultimately be stored. In fact

Figure 292:
An example of a personalised building.
(*Mark Densham*)

I have been known to slightly adjust the overall dimensions of a building so that it would fit into a convenient box!

No matter how simple or complicated a building, I always create plans or at least a few sketches, diagrams, or constructional schematics around which to work. You'll notice that none of the plans in this book show dimensions: I have several reasons for this, not least that there are so many different wargame scales that it would be impossible to include dimensions for every scale of figure, particularly when figures from different manufacturers which claim to be the same scale seldom match. The only way to be certain that your buildings and figures look right together is to scale the plans so that a based figure from your chosen manufacturer looks as if it could actually pass through a door without banging its head, or shoot out of a window without having to stand on a box.

Converting the plans to match your figures is straightforward and involves a couple of simple calculations:

- The based wargame figure is represented by (a)
- The height of the based figure on the plan is represented by (b)
- The conversion percentage is represented by (c)
- The length of the line on the plan is represented by (d)
- The scaled line length is represented by (e)

So:

- Measure the height of one of your based foot figures (a), and then measure the height of the based figure on the plan (b).
- To find the conversion percentage (c), apply the following formula: $\frac{a}{b}$ x 100 = (c).
- To find the scaled dimension (e), use the formula: (d) x (c) = (e).

There are several options to create buildings from my plans: enlarge or reduce them on a copier, scan them and then apply the enlargement or reduction or if you don't want to risk damaging the book, carefully trace the plans and then enlarge or reduce the tracing.

Most buildings just consist of an open-topped box (the walls) and a lid (the roof), to which are added doors and windows; however, many wargamers are reluctant to make their own buildings, which is a pity because there is considerable satisfaction to be gained – as well as money to be saved – by making your own buildings. To demonstrate this, the first building project covered in this chapter is a simple medieval cottage.

PROJECT 22: A Saxon Building

This basic building can – with a little imagination – be used from early Saxon to late medieval times as well as in countless fantasy worlds. This project is actually two slightly different buildings but with the same thatched roof.

MATERIALS
- High density foam
- Balsa wood
- Thick card
- Fake fur

CONSTRUCTION
Resize the plan (Figure 293) so that a based figure will fit through the door, and then transfer the dimensions onto your chosen material.

Figure 293:
Plan for a simple village building.

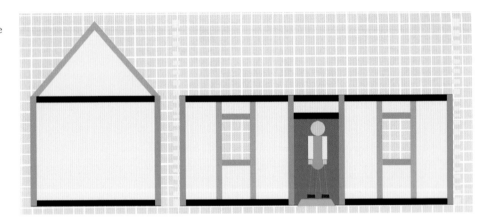

I used high density foam for the walls, but you could use foamboard, or cork tile. The plan shows one side and one end piece. You'll need two of each. I generally find it easier to cut out the doors and window apertures before cutting out the wall itself. Note that the feint dotted element indicates the position of the end walls when the building is assembled. End walls with a gable (pointed) end enclose the side walls.

Once the pieces are cut out the next step is to glue the side and end pieces together. It's not essential, but will improve the look of your building if you line the exposed areas of the high density foam with thin strips of balsa: for this project, that's the door and window frames (Figure 294). Next cut out the vertical timbers from balsa and glue them into place, and then add the remaining timbers (Figures 295–296).

Figure 294:
The building shell complete with lined apertures on the front wall.

Figure 295:
The building with the main vertical timbers added.

Figure 296:
The building complete with all the timbers.

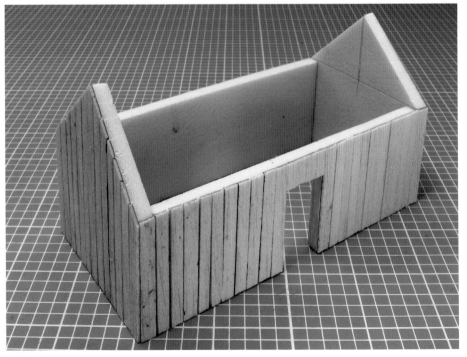

Figure 297:
An alternative style of building.

If you prefer to model a style of building with a completely timber construction without windows (such as reconstructions at the West Stow Anglo-Saxon village), don't cut out any window apertures and just clad the entire building with balsa planks. For more variation you can add a window or two, so there are plenty of ways to vary the appearance of your buildings (Figure 297).

Whichever style of building you choose, the construction of the thatched roof is the same. Taking dimensions from the building make a roof from thick card scored along the ridgeline so that it will fold neatly (Figure 298). If left unsupported the card roof would spring open so it needs something to stop this happening and also to prevent the finished roof sliding about. Draw a line along the underside of the roof where it will fit over the gables and using a pin vice, drill a series of holes the diameter of a small pin (Figure 299).

Cut two pieces of high density foam to the same shape as the triangular peak of the gable end, and glue them in position. To ensure that the roof doesn't spring open while the glue is setting, push pins through the roof into the foam at a slight angle. Once the glue has set, you may remove them, but I prefer to clip the heads off the pins and push them in so that the ends are flush with the roof surface (Figure 300). Ensure that the pins aren't too long otherwise they may protrude through the foam.

Figure 298: Measuring for the card roof.

219

Figure 299:
Drilling the roof.

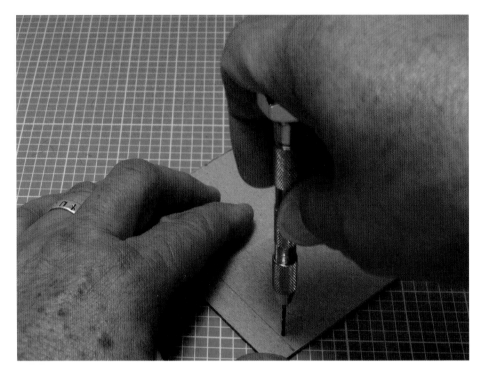

Figure 300:
A view showing the completed underside of the roof.

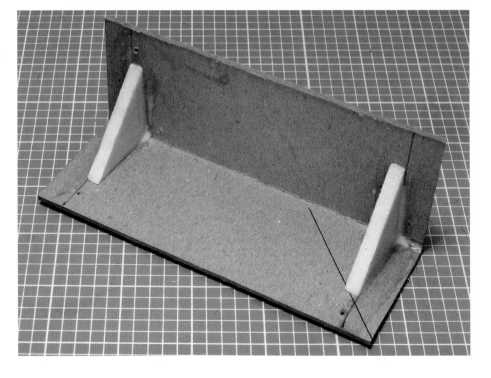

The thatch is simulated by using fake fur (Figure 301). First, cut two pieces oversize for each side of the roof. Fake fur naturally lies better in one direction than in another, so when you decide how to cut the fur, make sure that the direction in which the fur naturally lies is from the ridge of the roof down to the eaves. Glue the fur onto the roof using plenty of glue, then set it aside to dry thoroughly. This is particularly important because when you get to the next stage of combing the fur to give it the appearance of thatch: if it's not glued securely it will lift off, so use bulldog clips or other clamps to hold the fur firmly in place while the glue dries (Figure 302).

Coat the fur with slightly thinned PVA glue. You'll need to work it right into the fur and then, using a comb or something similar, comb the fur downwards from the ridge to the eaves (Figure 303). Once you're happy with the sides, cut a thin strip of fur and glue this along the ridgeline to hide the join between the two pieces (Figure 304). This can be fiddly because the fur only wants to lie in one direction whereas for the ridge ideally you want it to lay equally well in two opposite directions. My approach is to use a lot of glue that then allows you to gently pull the fur against its natural direction. Be warned though: it's a slow process.

The doors for the buildings are pieces of balsa cut to size and with the lines of the individual planks scored into the surface. The addition of a couple of cross beams adds to the realism of the doors (Figure 305). It can

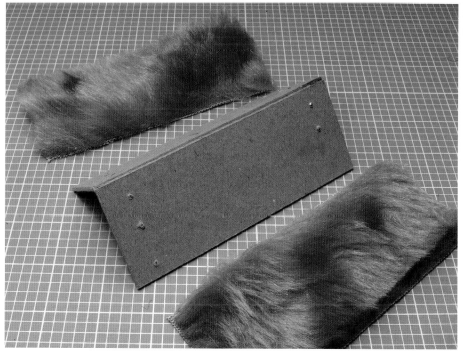

Figure 301:
The roof awaiting its fake fur thatch.

Figure 302:
A multitude of clips and clamps hold the fur in place.

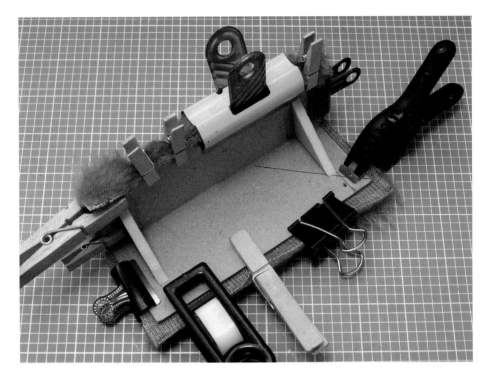

Figure 303:
Combing the fur.

Figure 304:
A basic thatched roof with ridge piece.

Figure 305:
A sample door.

Figure 306:
One painted building…

Figure 307:
…And a different painted building.

make it easier to fit the door securely if it's stuck onto a larger piece of balsa that can then be glued inside the building from behind.

The exterior plaster was painted a pale yellow, then drybrushed white. The wood was painted in black and drybrushed in pale grey. The thatch was first given a black undercoat, drybrushed dark brown and finally highlighted with pale yellow (Figure 306).

The second version of this building was slightly different because the outer walls were completely timbered, so there was no exposed plaster to be painted; otherwise the painting was the same (Figure 307). Once you've built one of these buildings, you can easily vary the dimensions or details to create an entire village, and the next project will show how to build a hall as a centrepiece for your village.

PROJECT 23: A Saxon Great Hall

The great hall was the focal point of most villages (Figure 308). It was where the lord of the manor or the village chieftain lived, and it was the venue for feasts and meetings. The construction materials varied considerably. The walls of the earliest halls were usually made from wattle and daub with roofs made from thatch or similar natural materials. Other options had the walls made from vertical wooden panels with a roof of wooden tiles or shingles. For this model I chose wattle and daub walls and a thatch roof, as I wanted to use it with my Romano-British hill fort (shown in Chapter Seventeen).

Figure 308:
The great hall in pride of place.

MATERIALS

- High density foam
- Balsa wood or coffee stirrers (balsa is easier to cut)
- Toothpicks
- Textured paper
- Thick card
- Coco fibre

You can use fake fur instead of coco fibre, as shown in the previous project (Figure 309).

CONSTRUCTION

Great halls varied considerably in size and proportion. Some were simply an enlarged version of a smaller building, and if that's the style of building you wish to create then you can use Project 22 earlier in this chapter as your starting point. However for something more dramatic, read on.

As usual, the first step is to create plans to match the scale of your figures (Figure 310). Cut out the walls and the door and any window apertures, and mark the positions for the timber uprights. Pin the walls together to ensure that you're happy with the proportions (Figure 311).

Figure 309:
A close-up of a fake fur roof.

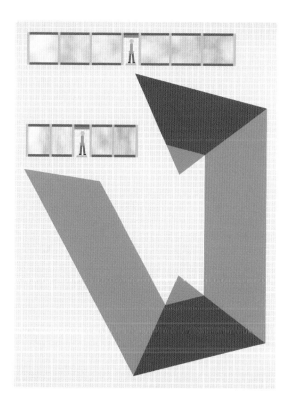

Figure 310:
Plan for the great hall.

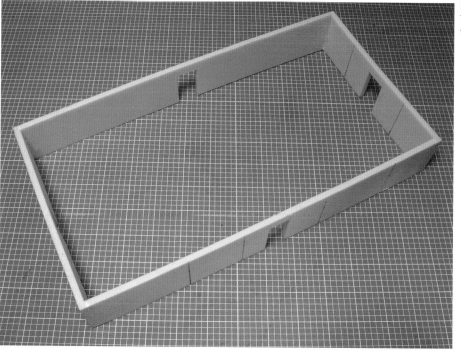

Figure 311:
The walls pinned together.

I prefer to base larger buildings to protect them. I normally allow about 2.5cm all around (Figure 312). Cut out your base from thick card, and pin and glue the walls onto the base (Figure 313). I was rather over-enthusiastic with the PVA glue so rather than waste the excess, I sprinkled on fine sand to give the ground some initial texture.

Next cut balsa strips for the timber uprights and glue them into position on the inside and outside of the walls. Add the horizontal beams, and give the base a coat of PVA glue and sprinkle on more patches of fine sand (Figure 314).

Paint the walls white and the timber black. You can leave the walls white if your building is intended to represent one that was recently constructed. However, I wanted my building to look somewhat shabby and well used, so I gave the buildings a dark brown wash (Figure 315). That's it for the walls for the time being.

Now let's take a look at the roof, which is a little more complicated than previous examples; however, if you study the photographs the assembly should be pretty obvious (Figures 316–317). The plans show the shape of the main part of the roof, which should be carefully cut out and scored to make it easier to fold it. Note that the upper triangles on the gables at each end have to be scored on the back so that they can be carefully folded into a perpendicular position. To finish off this supporting roof you need to cut

Figure 312:
The walls in position on the base.

Figure 313:
The walls pinned
to the base.

Figure 314:
Horizontal beams
added.

Figure 315:
The walls are given a dark wash.

Figure 316:
The card supporting roof, folded and glued together.

another length of thick card to form the ridge of the roof. Once you have started to create your building, use your plans as a general guide, but take precise measurements from the model itself.

Note the four pieces of card positioned to fit within the perpendicular end triangles of the roof and hold them in place. This ridge roof piece is glued to the main roof (Figure 318).

Most modelmakers have their preferred material for representing thatch; I usually use fake fur glued to a thick card supporting roof, coated with PVA and combed until it has the regular appearance of thatch. However for this building I decided to use coco fibre instead (Figure 319). It's quite thick but can be easily pulled apart to make a thinner layer.

Once you have thinned out the coco fibre, cut it to shape to match the individual panels of your roof and glue them into position (Figure 320). Continue cutting out your thatch sections and gluing them to the supporting roof with PVA glue (Figure 321). To make certain that the thatch is firmly attached, I also stipple PVA glue into the outer surface of the coco fibre.

You could leave the coco fibre unpainted, but I gave my roof a black undercoat, followed by a dark brown drybrush, finishing off with a very light drybrush of very pale yellow (Figure 322). It will take several days for the glue to completely dry: don't be tempted to start painting it too soon.

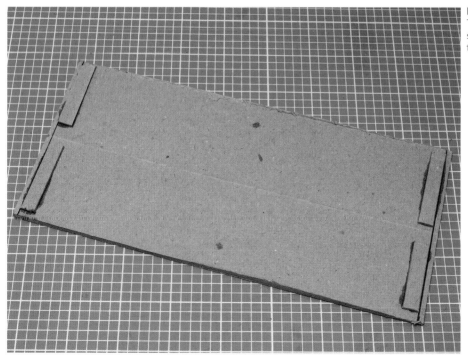

Figure 317:
The upper roof section that forms the ridge.

Figure 318:
The completed
supporting roof.

Figure 319:
Thinning out the
coco fibre.

Figure 320:
The first piece of thatch glued in place.

Figure 321:
All of the thatch glued in place.

Figure 322:
You could leave
the coco fibre
unpainted but I
decided to paint
mine.

Figure 322:
You could leave the coco fibre unpainted but I decided to paint mine.

For several reasons, I wanted to have access to the interior of the great hall. Potentially this is a big building compared to the others on your wargames table, and it takes up quite a lot of the playing area: if you don't have access to the building it basically becomes an obstacle around which your troops have to manoeuvre rather than a part of the game itself.

The lord's private quarters needed to be separated from the remainder of the great hall, which was often achieved by wattle screens; the plan shows the construction principle for creating these wattle screens (Figure 323). The construction steps are very simple: cut a piece of thin textured card to the size of your screen panel and then make a series of parallel cuts taking care not to cut right to the edges of the material (Figure 324). To make sure that you've cut all the way through, carefully slide a blade along each slit, taking care to work away from yourself of course. Carefully interweave cocktail sticks or toothpicks to create the wattle panel effect (Figure 325). It's always a good idea to make more panels than you think you're likely to need in case you damage any of them. To complete the construction of the panels, trim off the excess cocktail sticks, and add reinforcing pieces to the ends, cut from balsa strip (Figure 326). Give them a black undercoat followed by a grey drybrush. Give the base a brown undercoat both within the great hall and outside, and then glue the wattle screens in position (Figure 327).

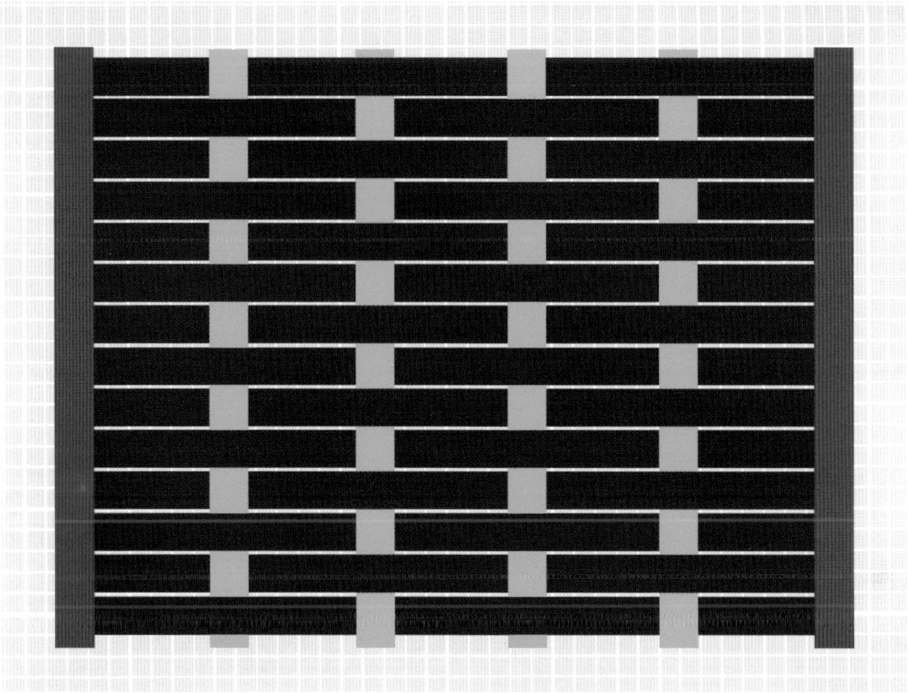

Figure 323:
The wattle screen.

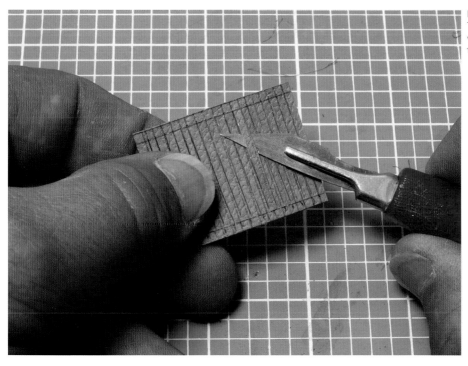

Figure 324:
The textured card
with slots cut to
take the uprights.

Figure 325:
A batch of wattle panels partially constructed.

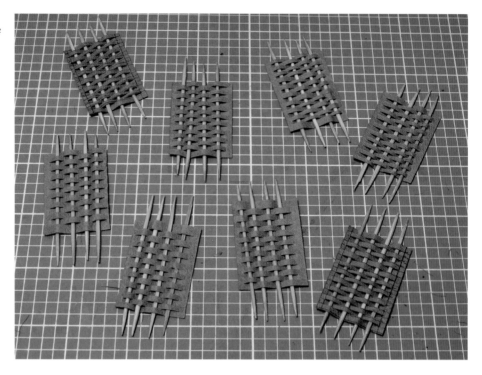

Figure 326:
The completed wattle panels.

Figure 327:
The wattle panels
glued in position.

The floor of a great hall in this period would probably have been covered with straw. To represent this I painted thinned PVA glue onto the floor area and sprinkled on finely cut pieces of coco fibre (Figure 328). It's a slow (and messy) process because you need to push the fibre into the glue so that it thoroughly absorbs it. Take this process slowly: too much glue and the floor may warp.

After giving the ground outside the great hall a light cream drybrush, brush PVA glue onto the areas where you want to create grass and sprinkle it on (Figure 329). Make some short planks from balsa. Paint them black followed by a grey drybrush and glue them in front of each doorway (Figure 330). The final touches are to make the main doors, which are simply pieces of balsa scored to represent planks, painted black and drybrushed grey.

If you decide that you want to add furniture or other items inside, it's probably not worth making your own because this can be fiddly and there are several manufacturers producing very good accessories. If you're having difficulty finding what you want, take a look in the roleplaying section of catalogues: you'll be surprised what you can find! I decided not to include any interior detail because I didn't want it to get in the way of gameplay.

Figure 328:
The straw is sprinkled in place.

Figure 329:
Static grass is added, leaving space for the wooden walkways.

Figure 330:
A walkway is a vast
improvement on
wading through
mud!

PROJECT 24: Half-timbered Buildings

Half-timbered buildings are the epitome of the multi-period building. They span hundreds of years and can be found in various forms all over Europe. And of course they can be used for fantasy as well as historical games.

These buildings are easily recognisable: the inner and outer walls comprise timber frames with the space between them being filled with various materials including wattle and daub, plaster or brick. The roofs were steeply pitched, primarily because they were originally thatched and a steep angle was necessary to prevent water lying on the roof and rotting through. Another advantage of the steeply pitched roof was that it provided a usable roof space, which was important in towns where building space was limited. As building methods changed, thatched roofs were frequently replaced by tiled ones but the pitch of the roof seldom changed.

To create simple variations in your half-timbered buildings, you can make the roofs for your buildings detachable so you can switch between thatched or tiled roofs. Another characteristic feature of half-timbered buildings was that often the upper floor, or floors were jettied (projected forward), which can be easily recreated and is demonstrated in this project.

All the buildings in this project can easily be adapted so long as you follow the basic construction techniques. In very general terms, there are two styles of buildings: those with the gable at the sides (which means that the ridgeline runs from left to right), and those with the gable at the front and rear (in which case the ridgeline runs from front to back).

MATERIALS

- Cork tiles
- Balsa
- Various thicknesses of card
- DAS Pronto air-drying clay.

Before getting started on the construction, a brief word about the materials: I'm always trying out different materials and for this project I decided to use cork tiles as the basis for the building, primarily because they have an interesting surface texture, but you can as easily use high density foam or foamboard.

CONSTRUCTION

The first step is to create plans to suit your scale of figure, by resizing the plans to match a based figure (Figure 331). As a first step towards personalising

Figure 331:
Plan for a half-timbered building.

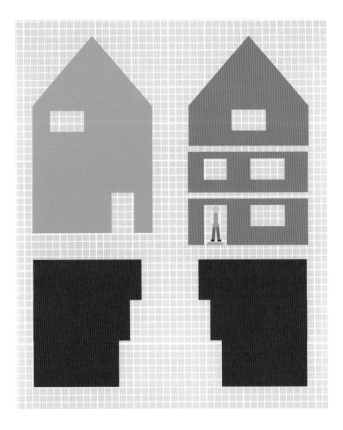

Figure 332:
Rear and side walls
showing floor
supports.

your half-timbered buildings, you can add, remove or reposition windows. It looks better overall if you keep the windows on each storey vertically aligned … and it makes it easier to add the timbers too.

Cut out the walls, and also make some floor supports from spare strips of cork and glue them in place (Figure 332). You don't have to stick with the position or number of windows shown because there's no right or wrong configuration. The only consideration is that if you're intending to butt buildings up against one another to make a long row, you might decide not to bother with windows in the side walls. Glue the back wall to one of the side walls (Figure 333). As ever, I'm a confirmed user of Lego bricks to create right angles.

The next stage is to add the floors. It's not practical to specify the dimensions of this component because inevitably this will depend on the scale of the building and the thickness of the construction material being used, so the most accurate method is to take your measurements from the model itself. The plan view (Figure 334) shows how the walls and floors fit together, and where on the model to take the measurements for the floor.

Cut out your floors and test fit them before gluing. Trim if necessary. Glue the other end wall into position taking care to ensure that the floors sit on the supports (Figure 335). Next glue the three front walls into place (Figures 336–337). Note that before gluing these in position I mark some guidelines for the vertical timbering.

241

Figure 333:
Glue the back and one end wall together.

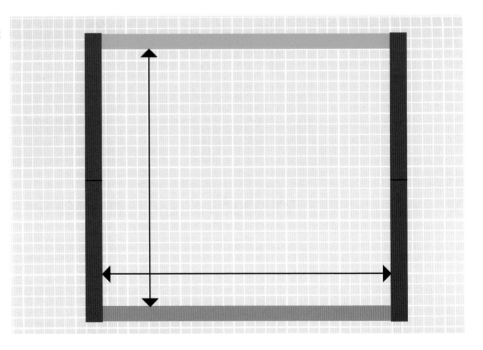

Figure 334:
Plan view showing how the floor fits within the outer walls.

Figure 335:
The two floors
glued in position.

Figure 336:
Rear and side walls
glued in place with
the floors also
fitted.

Figure 337:
The three front
walls glued to the
side walls.

Figure 338:
Adding the first
timbers.

244

Figure 339:
Adding the main
vertical timbers.

Figure 340:
The timbering for
the ground floor.

With the basic building constructed, the next stage is to add the timber framing. The pattern of framing varied from building to building, but as a general rule it looks better if all the vertical timbers line up on each storey.

The first timbers to be added were the uppermost horizontal timbers that will fit beneath the eaves (Figure 338). Next to be glued in position are the vertical timbers that form the edges of the jettied floors and the main upright that runs the full height of the building (Figure 339). The vertical and horizontal timbers for the ground floor were then glued into place (Figure 340). Next the timber framing for the first floor was positioned (Figure 341), and to complete the front of the building, the upper floor framing and the framing for the gable was glued into place (Figure 342).

Additional bracing beams were added, as well as the timbers to support the jettied upper floors. I also added doors made from pieces of balsa sheet with the appearance of planking created by ruling in vertical lines with an old ballpoint pen (Figure 343).

Note the position, or rather the angle, of the window bars. Before the introduction of leaded glass windows, the window aperture featured wooden bars, which, contrary to how they are often depicted, were often positioned at an angle as demonstrated in the following photograph taken at the Weald and Downland Open Air Museum, West Sussex (Figure 344). I have concentrated on the timbering for the front of the building, but the sides and rear of the building had simplified timber framing (Figure 345).

Figure 341:
Timbering for the first floor.

Figure 342:
The completed
first floor
timbering.

Figure 343:
Additional
timbering and
doors.

Figure 344:
The window bars.

Figure 345:
View showing the simplified timber framing on the side.

The next stage is to make the roof. As already suggested, it can add variety to your buildings if you have a choice of roofs available, which means that the roofs themselves must be removable. Each roof starts with a supporting roof made from thick card scored along the ridgeline so that it will fold cleanly (Figure 346). It will save time if you use black card because you won't have to paint the underside of the card where it overhangs the walls to form the eaves.

To ensure the roof retains the right pitch you need to cut some supports with the same profile as the gable end and glue them to the underside of the roof taking care that they are fitted away from the ends where the roof will rest on the gables (Figure 347). I augment the gluing of the supports by drilling holes through the card and pushing short pins through into the foam.

Next up is the chimney stack. Now, there's no such thing as a standard chimney stack; in fact in Victorian times when the first mass produced housing appeared, many builders used the chimney stack as a way of retaining individuality. From a modelling point of view, the way in which you build your chimneys depends on whether you want them to be attached to the roof, or extend them from the uppermost floor. If you choose the second option, this means that you will have to cut a fairly accurate hole in the roof, but the chimney stack will be more secure; this is the technique I adopt for buildings with particularly tall chimney stacks. The photograph (Figure 348) shows two such buildings under construction with their chimney stacks built into the outer walls and supported by the upper floor.

Figure 346:
Supporting roof
scored along
ridgeline.

Figure 347:
Triangular supports to hold the roof at correct angle.

Figure 348:
Tall chimney stacks need to be built into the outer walls and supported.

The chimney stack for this particular model is not very tall and it fits directly onto the roof which means that its lower edges must match the roof's pitch (Figure 349). Cut out the individual parts (Figure 350), and glue together one wide, and two narrow sides (Figure 351). Glue the remaining side in place and once dry, trim off any excess to ensure it fits the roof neatly (Figure 352).

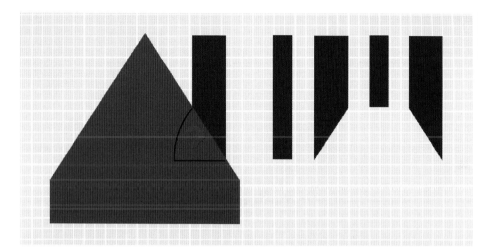

Figure 349: Determining the angle for the base of a chimney stack.

Figure 350: The chimney stack components.

Figure 351:
The chimney stack partially assembled.

Figure 352:
Trimming the chimney stack.

My method of simulating the chimney brickwork is to first coat it with Das Pronto air-drying clay and then engrave the brickwork using an old scalpel blade (Figure 353). Before starting to engrave the bricks, you should smooth the clay to create a good surface onto which to work. One useful tip is instead of just moistening the scalpel blade with water, dip it into a 50/50 water and PVA solution, because as the glue dries this helps to toughen the surface of the clay.

With the chimney stack completed, the next step is to add the roof tiles. This can be a laborious task, particularly if you apply the tiles individually. However, I now make strips of tiles and this is much quicker; the illustration (Figure 354) shows the principle. I create the grid for my tile strips on my computer, but you can just glue graph paper to a piece of thin card instead and use the squares as your guide.

I started tiling on the roof side without the chimney stack. Glue successive strips of tiles to the supporting roof (Figure 355). With that side completed, carefully position the chimney stack and draw around it; repeat the tiling process, avoiding the point where the chimney stack will be positioned (Figure 356). To make the securest fitting possible, drill a series of holes through the roof just inside this line. Glue the chimney stack in position and push pins through the roof from the underside to hold the chimney securely (Figure 357). Note that for this side of the roof I cut out some of the tiles and positioned them at an angle to suggest a few slipped or damaged tiles.

Figure 353: A close-up of chimney stack brickwork.

Figure 354:
How to make tiles
in strips.

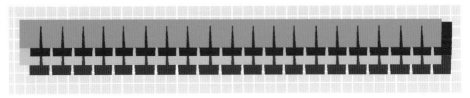

Figure 355:
One side of the
tiled roof.

The next stage is to paint the building. I nearly always undercoat my buildings in black and drybrush them as required. In this case, the building received a drybrush of grey to pick out the detail of the wood (Figure 358). Although the roof is separate from the building, I always prefer to paint the entire building at the same time. Next I picked out the plaster infill areas in white, and drybrushed the roof tiles in a brick red, picking out some tiles in a lighter tone of the same colour (Figure 359).

When I returned to the building after leaving it to dry thoroughly, I decided that it looked too 'chocolate-boxy': too clean, too neat. On a whim, I gave the building a brush over with Army Painter Strong Tone Quick Shade. I'd had some lying around for a while and had never plucked up the courage to use it on my figures, but thought that the buildings would be a good way to use it. The end result certainly toned the colours down (Figure 360)!

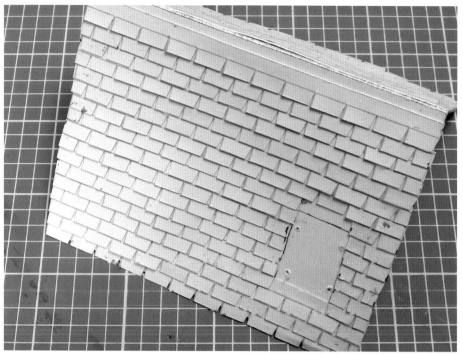

Figure 356:
The other side of the roof, with cut-out for chimney stack.

Figure 357:
The completed roof.

Figure 360:
The finished building after a wash of Army Painter Strong Tone Quick Shade.

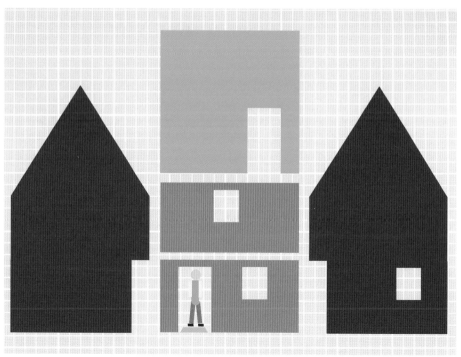

Figure 361:
An alternative half-timbered building design.

Figure 362:
Yet another
alternative building
design.

With minimal adaptations to the basic plans, you can create many different buildings with their own individuality (Figures 361–362). One of the most obvious variations is to have the ridgeline running from left to right instead of front to back, which means that the gables will be on each end.

The assembly procedure follows a similar sequence as before: the gable ended walls enclose the other walls, the side and rear walls are glued together and the floors are slid into position. The front walls are glued in place, and the timber framing is added. The chimney is constructed, the roof is tiled, the window bars and doors are added and the model is painted.

PROJECT 25: A Yarn Market

This project is inspired by the yarn market at Dunster in Somerset (Figure 363), close to where I live. It was built around 1590 by George Lutrell, and was designed to shelter fabric traders and their goods from the elements. The original building has a large overhanging roof to offer shelter to customers viewing the goods. As a model, the yarn market makes a good centrepiece, but the construction of this octagonal building is not for the faint hearted, although it is relatively straightforward if you take your time.

MATERIALS
- Cork tiles
- Thick card or mounting board
- Thin card
- Textured wallpaper

CONSTRUCTION
The first step is to construct an octagonal template for the base and the underside of the roof (Figure 364). You'll need a compass and a ruler.

- Draw a square the size of your required octagon onto a piece of thick card or mounting board, and connect the corners to create the diagonals and find the centre point.
- Divide the square into eighths by drawing a horizontal and vertical line through the centre.
- Draw a circle with a radius set to half the width of the box.
- Connect the points where the circle crosses the lines to create your octagon.

Cut out two of these octagons from cork tile or high density foam. Glue cobblestone effect textured wallpaper to both sides of one octagon. The reason for gluing it to both sides is to prevent warping, which may happen if you only glue the wallpaper to one side (Figure 365).

259

Figure 364:
Constructing an octagon.

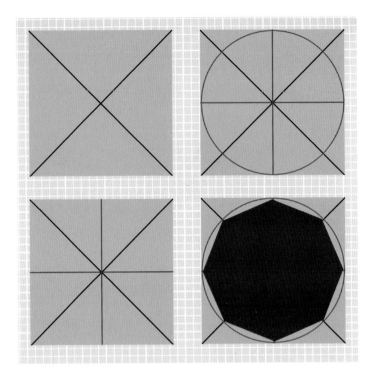

Figure 365:
The yarn market base with textured wallpaper.

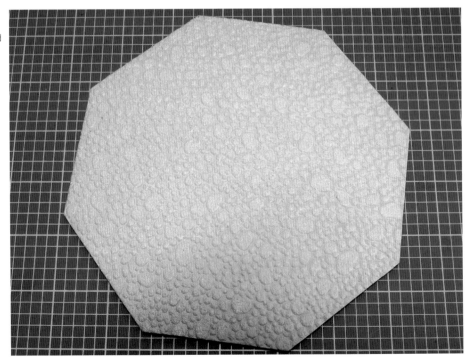

The yarn market has a wall around its outer edge with a single opening for access. The walls are made from two thicknesses of cork tile, but with the innermost layer slightly shallower to create a step. You'll need to clamp the cork sections together for 24 hours to ensure a good lamination (Figure 366).

Due to the octagonal shape, the end of each wall section must be cut at an angle so that they all butt up perfectly. I found that the easiest method was to lightly draw a line between each opposite corner of the octagon and then cut the first wall section roughly to size; hold it in position and trim the ends by cutting vertically downwards using the lines as a guide. Glue this first wall section in position (Figure 367). The remaining walls are cut to size by butting one end up to the previous wall and then trimming the other to match the drawn guide lines. Glue each wall section into place and fill any gaps as necessary (Figure 368). Cut strips of textured wallpaper and glue them to the inner and outer surfaces of the wall (Figure 369). The basic walls are finished off by adding card pieces along the upper edge to simulate stone slabs (Figure 370).

Figure 366:
The inner and outer wall pieces clamped together.

Figure 367:
Fitting the first wall.

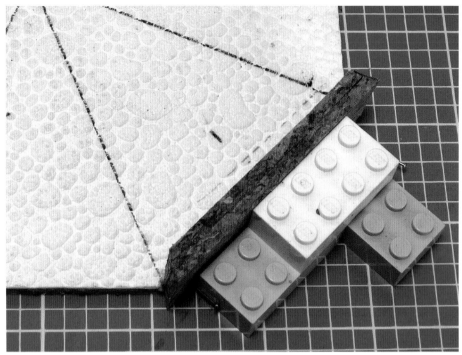

Figure 368:
The other walls in place.

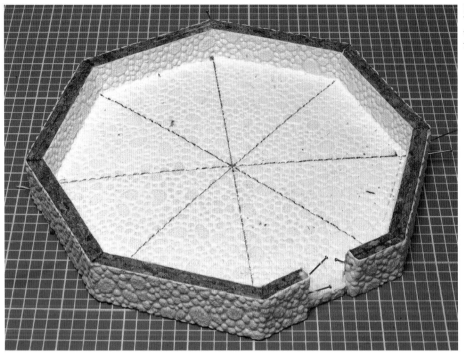

Figure 369:
The walls covered with cobble effect textured wallpaper.

Figure 370:
Capping the walls with stone slabs.

The yarn market roof uses the second octagon. Carefully draw guidelines on one side linking the opposite corners (Figure 371). As if the octagonal shape wasn't enough of a challenge, construction of the roof needs a bit of extra thought too! Eventually I decided upon a full width profile piece (Figure 372), to which would be fitted spoke-like shorter angled pieces. I used balsa sheet for my profiles rather than cork, because I felt that the cork was too thick. First the full width profile piece was glued in place (Figure 373). Next, take another profile piece and cut it in half. Take one half and trim the innermost edge until it butts up to the first profile piece and lines up with the edge of the roof, and then glue it into position (Figure 374). Trim the other half as necessary and glue it in place (Figure 375). You need another four roof profiles, so follow the same procedure (Figure 376). Because of the thickness of the material, make these the same size as the preceding ones but gradually trim them until they fit.

The roof is surmounted by a cupola that needs a base on which to stand, so cut a small octagonal piece of balsa and glue it on top of the profiles (Figure 377). Each of the eight roof segments features a window to help illuminate the area beneath the yarn market roof. The plan shows the general shape of this component but to be accurate, take measurements from the model itself (Figure 378). Obviously you'll need eight of these window panels, but unless the assembly of your roof so far has been incredibly precise, each

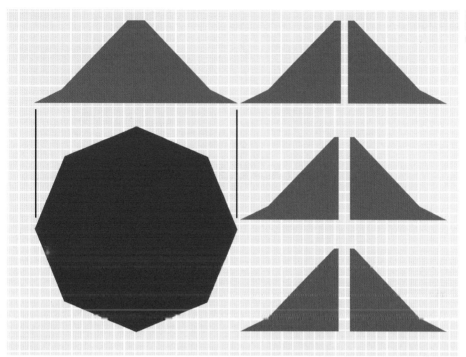

Figure 372:
Plan for the basic
roof components.

Figure 373:
The first stage in
building the roof.

Figure 374:
Adding the first half profiles.

Figure 375:
The other half profile in position.

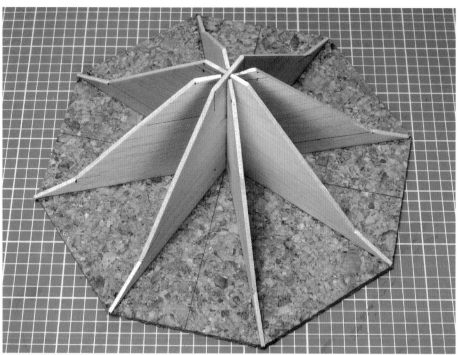

Figure 376:
Completing the
roof profiles.

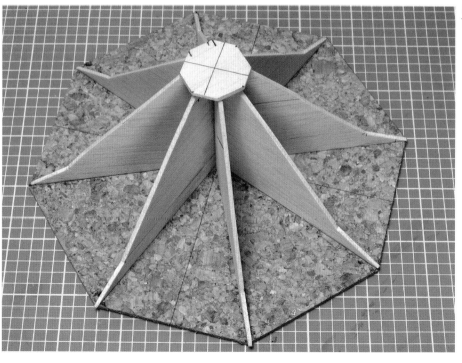

Figure 377:
The cupola base.

Figure 378:
Plan for the window panel.

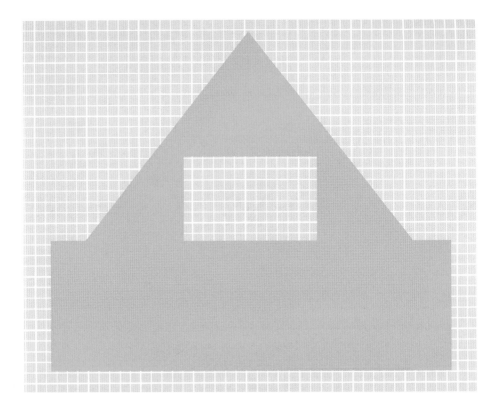

Figure 379:
The first window panel in place.

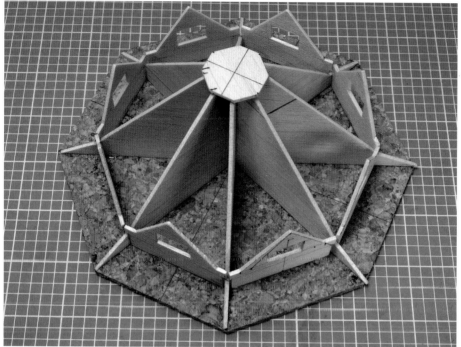

Figure 380:
The remaining
window panels
glued to the roof
profile pieces.

of the roof sections will be slightly different so you'll have to measure each one. Start by gluing the first panel in position (Figure 379). I used a piece of scrap balsa to push the lower edge inwards to get the panel vertical. Taking measurements from the model, make the remaining seven window panels and glue them to the roof profile pieces (Figure 380).

The roof of the yarn market is split into the lower and upper sections. Both sections are tiled but first they need a supporting roof. The dimensions for these roof sections must be taken from the model. Working one by one, measure, cut out, and glue each lower roof support in place (Figure 381). I made mine from balsa.

The upper roof also needs supporting pieces for the tiles, which are made from individual pieces of card glued to the roof profiles (Figure 382). I used card instead of balsa because the thickness of the balsa made it difficult to get a neat join between the roof panels at the top. The tiles are made from strips of thin card that are partially cut to create gaps between the individual tiles (Figure 383). These tile strips were created on my computer, but an alternative method is to glue graph paper to thin card and use the squares of the graph paper as the grid. Start by adding the lower line of tiles all the way around the lower roof (Figure 384). For the subsequent rows the process is basically the same: cut a strip of tiles to the width of the supporting roof and angle the ends to match the taper of the roof. Work your way around

Figure 381:
The lower roof sections in place.

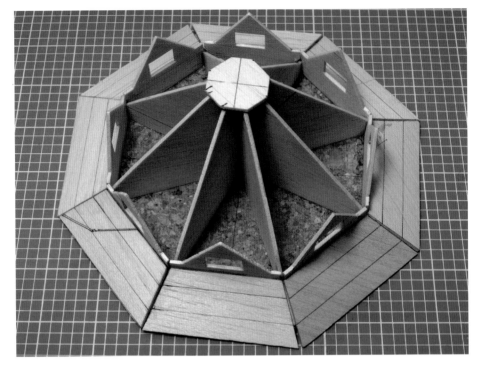

Figure 382:
The upper roof sections in place.

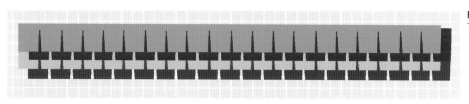

the roof to complete that line of tiles before proceeding to the row above. Continue until the lower roof is completed (Figure 385). The upper roof follows the same procedure (Figure 386).

Each gabled window also needs a supporting roof, which is made from a piece of folded card. As usual, take measurements from the model (Figure 387). If you want your model to have leaded windows they must be added at this point by cutting small pieces of aluminium mesh, spraying them black, and gluing them behind the window panel.

Add tiles to the gable roofs following the same procedure already covered for the lower and upper roofs (Figure 388). Next the windows in the gables need to have outer frames added from balsa strip (Figure 389). To complete the windows, carefully add the bars (Figure 390).

Making the rooftop cupola is the next stage. The roof of the cupola is made from an octagonal piece of balsa, a card supporting roof and a

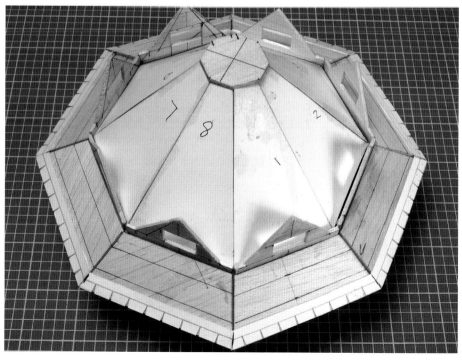

Figure 384:
The upper roof sections in place.

271

Figure 385:
The lower roof
completely tiled…

Figure 386:
…And the upper
roof tiled.

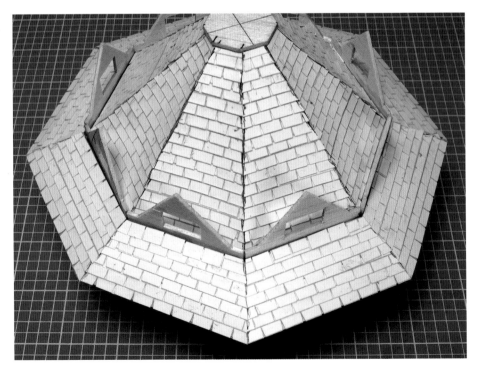

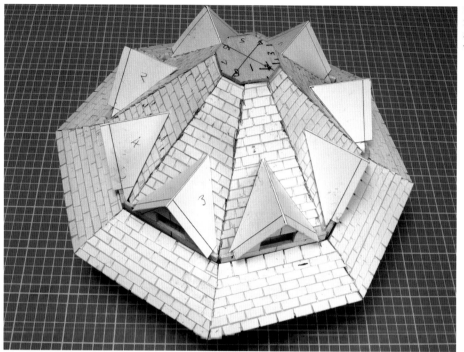

Figure 387:
Supporting roofs added to the gable windows.

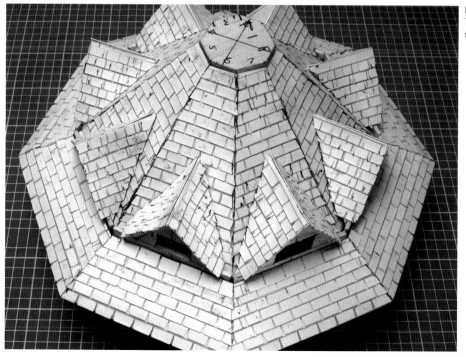

Figure 388:
The eight gable roofs tiled.

273

Figure 389:
Adding the
window frames to
the gable windows.

Figure 390:
Window bars in
place.

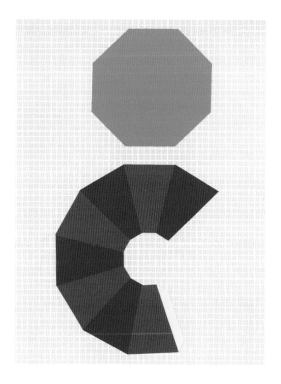

Figure 392:
Plan for the
cupola's roof.

wooden bead (Figure 391). The cupola roof itself needs a supporting roof made from folded card. You need to create a plan which takes the length of one side of the cupola base for the base width for each of the eight panels (Figure 392). This is a bit of trial-and-error. Once you're happy with the shape of the cupola roof, glue it together and add the wooden bead to finish it off; like all the other roofs this one needs tiling using the technique already covered (Figure 394). The cupola has a small surrounding wall on the base, which is made from strips of balsa glued around the edge (Figure 395). The cupola roof supports are also cut from strips of balsa; I started with four supports to hold the cupola roof and then added the remaining four once the cupola roof was in place (Figure 396).

With the cupola assembly in place, give the roof assembly a black undercoat followed by a grey drybrush (Figure 397). Usually I prefer to completely assemble my models prior to painting, but it would be impossible to paint the underside of the roof once it was joined to the base. I picked out random tiles in a lighter grey and also painted the ridges on the gable roofs in a contrasting colour (Figure 398).

Although the main roof will be supported around its perimeter, the Dunster yarn market also has an octagonal central pillar to support it. It's not strictly necessary to make this for the model, because it's difficult to see much underneath the roof, but I decided to make one anyway to make the

Figure 393:
The cupola's supporting roof assembled.

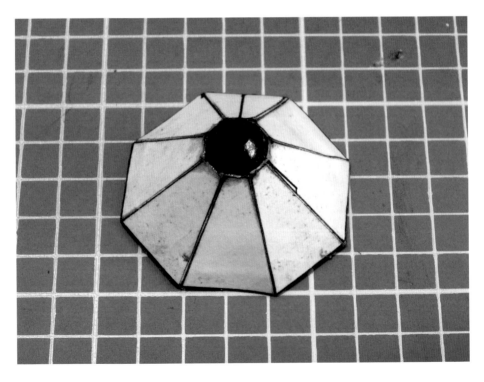

Figure 394:
The tiles added.

Figure 395:
The cupola's base wall.

Figure 396:
The initial cupola
roof supports.

Figure 397:
The completed
roof assembly
undercoated and
drybrushed.

Figure 398:
More detail picked
out on the roof.

model more sturdy. I used the octagon created for the cupola to save me having to make another template. Cut out two octagons from high density foam. Next cut eight pieces of balsa to make the sides of the octagonal pillar; this involves a bit trial and error because their width will depend upon the thickness of the material itself (Figure 399). The height is easier to determine: make it high enough so that there's plenty of room for a based figure to stand underneath. I made my column sides 4cm high.

Lay one pillar piece on its side and glue an octagon at each end (Figure 400). Once the glue has dried, carefully turn the octagons round one face and glue another side piece in position. Once all the sides have been glued in position, glue it to the underside of the roof assembly (Figure 401). Cut a strip of textured wallpaper to same height as the pillar and glue it around the pillar. Now is a good time to paint the underside of the roof and pillar because it will be impossible to do so once the roof assembly is glued in place.

Figure 399:
Two octagons
and eight panels
required.

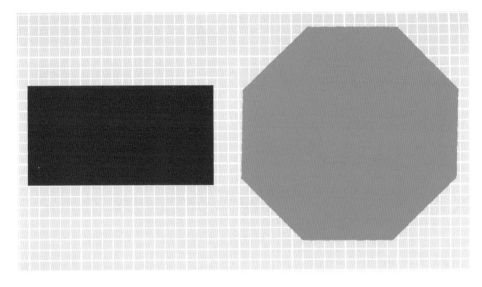

Figure 400:
The supporting
pillar, part
way through
construction.

Figure 401:
The octagonal central pillar glued in place.

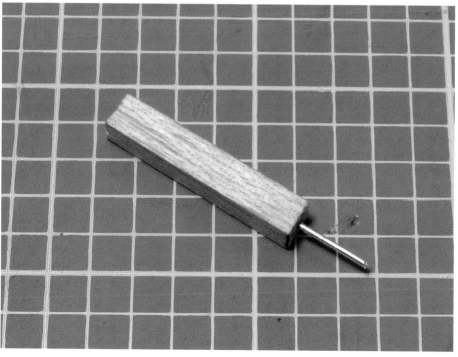

Figure 402:
A roof supporting pillar.

The next stage is to create the supporting pillars that join the roof to the base (Figure 402). These are made from square section balsa. To make a really strong joint, I drilled carefully into the end of the pillar and inserted a pin, clipping off the head. The first pillar is pinned and glued to one side of the opening (Figure 403); fit the remaining pillars and give the base a black undercoat followed by a grey drybrush (Figure 404). Pick out random stones to break up the grey. Once satisfied with the overall look, glue the roof and base together. With the model assembled, carefully pick out the area surrounding the gable windows in pale yellow or white to simulate plaster (Figure 405).

As mentioned at the start of this project, the yarn market is quite an involved building to construct – but all the more rewarding and satisfying for that reason – and so it's a fitting model with which to end this book, which will hopefully provide inspiration and give you a few ideas to get started or to help you develop your own terrain and scenery making.

Figure 403:
The first pillar to support the roof is positioned.

Acknowledgements and Thanks

Thanks to my work with *Wargames Illustrated*, I've had the opportunity to visit numerous wargame shows in the UK over the years, and have been able to see the very best that our hobby has to offer. I'd like to thank all those wargamers and modelmakers who have demonstrated their amazing talent and skills to inspire us, a very small percentage of whose masterpieces appear within the pages of this book. I have tried extremely hard to correctly credit all the photographs, but sincere apologies for any errors or omissions, which are of course totally down to me.

I'd also like to express my thanks to those wargamers who patiently stopped their games to allow me to take my photographs, and to the show organisers who have, without exception, always made me feel welcome at their events.

But our hobby is not just about the wargamers. We are fortunate to have some excellent manufacturers and traders around, many of whom are also wargamers. Because of their efforts, enthusiasm, and more recently the Kickstarter concept, it becomes increasingly difficult to find a wargame subject – be it historical, fantasy or sci-fi – for which figures are not available. Several manufacturers have been particularly helpful by donating products to help in the production of this book, and I'd like to make a point of thanking:

- Heroics & Ros Miniatures
- Magister Militum
- Perry Miniatures
- Spartan Games
- Warlord Games

Many of the photographs of the completed terrain and scenery in this book would have been impossible without the generosity of my friends at the Minehead Wargames Club: Mark, Roger, Dan and Nik, who were more than happy to make their figures available to me, so a special thank you to all of them.

Finally, last but definitely not least, I must thank my wife Joanne and son Sebastian for putting up with the chaos associated with creating this book. As the deadline for submitting the manuscript approached (and which I missed, sorry Phil), there was hardly a room in our house that didn't have it's share of partially completed models or scenery, as well as scraps of balsa, card, cork tile, pins and even in some cases a fine coating of foam dust. I'll try to be a lot tidier when I write the next one … honest.

Index

This index lists selected text and photographs. Unsurprisingly in a practical book such as this, it is impossible to list every subject and every photograph.

Please note that numbers in *italics* refer to photographs.

285